MARRIAGE UnBREAKABLE

JERMAEL & CARRIE ANTHONY

Marriage UnBreakable

Copyright © 2017 by Kingdom at Hand Ministries
P.O. Box 21575
Chicago, IL 60621

Published 2017 by Jermael and Carrie Anthony

All rights reserved. No portion of this book may be reproduced, photocopied, stored, or transmitted in any form-except by prior approval of publisher.

Unless otherwise noted, all Scripture quotations are taken from the **New King James Version** of the Bible.

Cover design by: Rebeca Covers

Book Layout by: www.diverseskillcenter.com

Published by: Kingdom at Hand Int. Ministries

Printed in the United States of America

ISBN: 978-0692925348

ISBN: 0692925341

Dedication

We would like to thank our parents whom between all three marriages there were about ninety years of marriage. Your examples set the tone for what created our household and we are appreciative of you. We have learned remarkable life lessons to press and serve God and hold personal relationships with God so that we have a firm foundation to build our home upon. ***To you: Darrell and Myrtis, (Honoring the Late William Howard Daniels) and Malikah, Jerry and (Honoring the Late Lee Ander [Teeny] Anthony)***

To the Oompa Loompas: We love you greatly, passionately and unconditionally. Josiah, Kai and Myah: it is continuously our prayer that you marry spouses, that love you the way Christ loved the Church and sacrificed Himself, be submitted to God and your particular family visions and build. Know that marriage will have its struggles, highs and lows but with Christ as the foundation and kept in the center of it all; He will keep your marriage. We decree healthy, longevity and stability into marriages in Jesus Name! We loose generational blessings; bind and cast out generational curses! In Jesus Name.

To Tapley Nation: Learn, Lean on and Grow UP together. Learn about and from one another. Lean on each other forever and grow up in Christ together! Never try to change one another, but embrace all of each other. This is the beginning of a beauty journey marked by joys and perils but enjoy every moment and thank Jesus for it all!

To Pastor Leonard and Dr. LeeChunHwa Stovall: We love and appreciate the: prayers, checkups, your ears and hearts. You are the glitter of promise fulfilled in the kingdom of God. We love you both!

To Bishop Nathaniel and Lady Tandeka Isaac: Bishop, we will be continuously appreciative, grateful and aware that God sent us you to *save our lives and marriage.* We have learned so much from you. Your presence in our lives has been nothing short of a miracle! Thank You!

To Apostle Malone and Lady Malone: Thank You Both, your example of marriage and labor in the Body of Christ is priceless. We appreciate each and every encounter! May many continue to change, grow and restore marriage because of your ministry!

To Predecessors: (Honoring the Late) Granddaddy Lovelace, Granddaddy Arthur, Grandmother Theresa, Great-Grandmother Carrie, Aunt Edna, Aunt Gladys and Uncle

Eric. Your presence and wisdom in my life is indescribable.

Table of Contents

Preface 9

The Original Intent of Marriage – In the Beginning.. 15

Healthy Marriages Creates Healthy Marriages. 33

Marriage Hopefuls... 71

Marital Warning.. 101

This Is What Marriage Looks Like 119

Satan's Lies Versus God's Truth 123

Breaking the Spirit of Adultery........................ 198

Contact Us 210

"Set me as a seal upon your heart, as a seal upon your arm, for love is strong as death, jealousy is fierce as the grave. Its flashes are flashes of fire, the very flame of the LORD. Many waters cannot quench love, neither can floods drown it. If a man offered for love all the wealth of his house, he would be utterly despised."

Song of Solomon 8:6-7 NKJV

Preface

We have seen throughout the years that marriages in the Body of Christ suffer and many in end divorce, much like sixty percent (60%). Our own marriage has taken detrimental hits (infidelity, job loss, possession lost and addictions); it is our desire to shed light and hope in marriages throughout the Body of Christ. In marriage, vows are tested and the very foundation of what you have felt in the beginning of the relationship is tested. However, though marriages experience many different seasons, trials and tribulations the sacred beauty and revelation of marriage still brings grace and mercy and a deeper understanding of just how much Jesus Christ loves us. We may commit wrongdoings against spouse(s), we may like the wrongdoings we commit (or endured), but Jesus, who lived a sinless existence, stands before God to take our place and responsibility for our failures. Jesus loves his Church with a great love. In return Jesus only desires for us to love and keep His commandments and *submit* to his Lordship. This is the same principle that has been instituted into the marriage in the beginning of mankind *after* the fall. Husbands lead and love your wives and wives in return submit to your own husbands having affections for him only. Nonetheless, this is the same principle that reflects the mystery of the beauty of marriage; which is only revealed after each individual enters into vows between God, husband and wife. When we carry out these principles we will begin to experience the blessings of Lord God upon our marriages in plethora of ways. These blessings come in ways of: longevity of union, love, peace, respect, wisdom, advice, rewards, learning, growing, evolving, prayers answered and good sex. God has intended that we enjoy our lives here as we live them. *"Behold that which I have seen: it is good and comely for one to eat and to drink, and to enjoy the good of all his labour that he taketh under the sun all the days of his life, which God giveth him: for it is his portion."* Ecclesiastes 5:18 King James Version. Why not enjoy life in your marriage too?! Marriage can be a glorious life built upon the foundation of the word of God, with structural beams of friendship completing the house with walls of love, ceilings of peace and floors of hope. We can experience the truth of God and the goodness of God through our spouses when we learn *the touch* of our spouses. The sole focus is to be obedient to the words of God and keep the covenantal vows you have made between: God, husband and wife. With these principles set forth and followed we too, in the Body of Christ can have joyful unions that are marked with peace, joy and righteousness in the Holy Spirit, which will spill over into our everyday lives and finances. When we begin to deeply understand the love of Jesus we then gain a greater understanding of the power that flows between the husband and wife. We also begin to see the undeniable strength that fastens the marriage together making it a firm, impenetrable force. We must first identify any remaining lusts. Lust is a destroyer of anything deemed holy. Just because you marry does not kill or satisfy lust. Take the time in transparency between you and your spouse to pinpoint areas of lust that hinder and block the flow of the love of God in your marriage and evict it out of your marriage. Once lust is evicted out of every area of your marriage ask God to overtake you both with the revelation of His love, this in turn will be the ruling force in your marriage and you will learn your spouse's *touch* and receive a greater tangible outpouring of blessings and revelation from heaven. This is the time for married couples to participate in having an unending relationship with heaven and earth, husband and wife and feel the love of God between you both!

The Original Intent of Marriage: In The Beginning

And God said, let us make man in our image, after our likeness: and let them have dominion over the fish of the sea, and over the fowl of the air, and over the cattle, and over all the earth, and over every creeping thing that creepeth upon the earth. So, God created man in his own image, in the image of God created he him; male and female created he them. And God blessed them, and God said unto them, be fruitful, and multiply, and replenish the earth, and subdue it: and have dominion over the fish of the sea, and over the fowl of the air, and over every living thing that moveth upon the earth.
And God said, Behold, I have given you every herb bearing seed, which is upon the face of all the earth, and every tree, in the which is the fruit of a tree yielding seed; to you it shall be for meat. And to every beast of the earth, and to every fowl of the air, and to everything that creepeth upon the earth, wherein there is life, I have given every green herb for meat: and it was so. And God saw everything that he had made, and, behold, it was very good. And the evening and the morning were the sixth day.
Genesis 1:26-31 King James Version

In the beginning God created: man, and woman, male and female he created them. He spoken male and female into existence one for another and blessed them, commanded they are fruitful and multiply together. When Adam had been physically created, (with Eve in mind and yet shut within Adam) he had given an initial command to Adam to shield and lead his family with a command, "Do not eat from the tree of..." This commandment from God is representing the leadership and trial of Adam. This would also begin to show Adam's: love and allegiance to either himself or his desires or to a Sovereign God. God did not desire to control Adam but desired that Adam would show temperance (self- control) and lead himself and his family. When Adam—transgressed **not** Eve: the finality of the covenantal command that God spoke over Adam seemingly irretrievably broken, the fall now affects all mankind. God had entered the judgment into existence that the wife should "Desire her husband only" and "I will put hatred between your Seed and his seed" and Adam "work by the sweat of his brow and the earth would not yield to him any longer." Let's get into what was occurring in that moment... Deep inside women there is a cry that she is the only one that can fulfill, satisfy, comfort, care and minister to her own husband. This component also is an alarm when something is going detrimentally wrong within the union. This yearning also heightens in marital duress and she still yearns for the affections of her husband still desires her husband though his affections may have soured. This is the judgmental command in effect. Adam: men are commanded to work but the earth will not yield to him. Meaning, husband will chase: success, monies, prestige, satisfaction, comfortable, virility and affirmation of being the provider of the home as well as experience the fleeting feeling of never meeting the goal. [This is the curse of the fall] Prior to the fall: Adam named every animal on the planet (meaning calling out its destiny, distinction and purpose) he also tilled the ground with ease and spoke to it and the ground would yield. Which causes men to inherit the blessing of being a problem solver from prior to the fall. At the point of the fall and thereafter, there is no more speaking and manifestation; but physical, emotional and mental hard labor to occur and even still the earth is resistant and rebellious to man's efforts. Instead of man's command husband now **needs** Jesus' assistance to catapult husband past the curse of judgment and into blessings and manifestation. Thus, he can work 80 hours a week and still feel useless and under paid.

Because the original command was not obeyed, both sides of humanity (*male* and *female*) have new commandments. They both will operate out of the curse of the judgment of the fall until accepting Jesus Christ, which breaks the curse of the fall. Though the effects of the curse is broken until the mentality of the fall has to be renewed or husband and wife will still operate out of the curse. Renewing the mind and breaking the curse will grant access to the blessings originally granted before the fall.

The working husband is not placed in the Bible as a metaphor, but is quite literal. Man is now commanded to work. He is not commanded to be lazy. He must work toiling the land by the sweat of his brow. When Adam was placed in the Garden of Eden his purpose was to: first dress it and second to keep it. The word *dress* in this scripture means to: serve, labor, work, and even to be led or enticed to serve. Originally, Eden was a place of:

perfect pleasure, delight, and luxury. This was the first manifestation of heaven on earth. Everything he needed was already there. So how was he to serve? Adam, a prototype, was the first father manifested as son and origin of God. As such his orders, even in a perfect place like Eden are to serve in three ways. First, he was to be the primary priest. Second, he was to be *the* leader of worship. Third he was to be the headmost person to cause things to manifest, or the initiator of faith. Reintegrating the previous statement: Adam's second command from God concerning Eden was to *keep it*. Scriptural meaning '*keep it*' is to protect it. Adam was to build a hedge around Eden, guard Eden, take care of Eden, preserve Eden, and ultimately save the life of Eden and all creatures that dwelled within. He was to be aware of every detail of Eden. Adam was supposed to be the original watchman. Being careful to observe all under his charge. This is the job description of Adam as well as every man on earth. This definitely sounds like **husband** work to me! Take note: Adam is a man and all men are *created* to be husbands. The *process* of *becoming* a man leads all men to become husbands. It is God's process of growth and development. Within the innate design of Adam was already a husband. He simply had not come into the fullness of his potential. When Adam was ready God gave him a wife. Such is the same even until today. God doesn't give wives to the undeveloped. So, if Adam was already a husband, who or what was he married to before he received Eve? Adam had given himself to God completely. He was married to the assignment and will of Our Father. Before any man has the awesome assignment of a wife, he must first steward over his first: calling, purpose, mission, area of influence, money, career, education or economic situation. Preparation in one's grooming process also means being happily single (unmarried) as well as steadily concerning himself with the role of priest, worshipper, and man of faith. It is my honest recommendation that those that desire to marry should take this preparation and promise time with the Lord first. Why? Because if you can't treat King of Kings and Lord of all right how can you treat your wife right?

Satan stole Adam's lifestyle. Adam watched as Satan enticed Eve to destroy the Government God had established at the helm of their creation. Meaning: the fall was done under the *leadership* of Adam.
Adam, just as beguiled, enticed and desperate as Eve ate of the tree they were *commanded* not to eat of. Suddenly both of their eyes were opened. Both Adam and Eve were

now rebellious toward God. They both digested nutrients of death and destruction and this rebellion opened up doors of wicked knowledge they were never created to know. The word *serpent* in this scripture means: subtle, whisper, magic spells, enchantment, learn by experience, diligently observe, observe signs, practice fortunetelling, or to practice divination. Neither Adam nor Eve foreknew this: subtle, cunning, evil spirit would bring all of this to their world. They were suddenly aware of and now made subject to all of these evil desires. Because they submitted to the serpent's enchantments, magic, deception and enticement illegitimate knowledge was born. Adam opened the doors to these systems and ideals. The knowledge of good and evil reigned as the illegal government. This means Adam gave the rights of sonship and the kingdoms of earth away, lost dominion and gained the power of sin, death and destruction because, *"it was pleasant to the eyes."* When this was done, Adam was cursed to work the fields *knowing* that his work will not produce satisfaction or appreciation but give rise to obligation. The perception of failure in one's heart, that no matter how hard he performs to succeed, he may never obtain success is discouraging. In addition: he could not protect the very thing left to his charge. Legally Adam could never obtain rights and privileges abdicated by loss and inner failure. On a daily basis men continue to hide leftover feelings from Adam's great fall. The fall of man not only changed Adam however, changed all of mankind for future generations to come. The deepest yearning of man is to regain the respect lost from failing his Creator. The Creator gave Adam freedom and law. Adam's freedoms and restraints encompassed his identity. Within freedom and law God relinquished to him: the freedom to ascend, elevate, command, and altogether rule—subject, take dominion. Freedom to take dominion over all living things was a huge task; nonetheless, this is what he was created for. Adam was created for greatness. Adam was created to lead Earth. This is the innate yearning and purpose of man; created to dominate but also made to submit. Adam's understanding was that his power came from his *position of submission*. After God made Adam and envisioned that his leadership was active; approval was written in God's heart and Word (And God saw everything that he had made, and, behold, *it was* very good. Gen 1:31 KJV.) At that point, Adam never needed to seek approval; approval and affirmation were Adam's vested interests. Inside of a single Man was the government of God. And God said this was good.

Over the spectrum of time, man walked with God in his divine purpose. God designed humankind for proximity to Him and was never designed to stray away onto a different course. The Father's original intent is that humankind would walk closely with Him gaining: definition, identity, and purpose. The walk with the Father then and now is the strength man's calling. Wrestling to spend time with the Father was never in the original make-up. Struggling to adhere to God's commandment was never in the original make-up. In fact, the commandment to not eat of the tree of the knowledge of good and evil was put into place to stop covetousness, lust, and pride. God knew of the dangers inside of His Garden. He knew that the original demonic force was hiding. Satan the deceiver (the serpent) had been in the garden since the beginning. The serpent was observant and subtil. He watched for as long as he needed to in order to find an opportunity.

God made woman because it was no longer good that man should be alone. God saw it fit to create a helpmeet for Adam. Now interestingly enough this helpmeet was designed to: surround, protect, and aid Adam. Woman's initial design was that of defense. The origin of woman is the rib of man. She is positioned to shield the heart. Woman was closest to the heart of man so she is able to discern it. But her main job is to protect the man's heart, mind, will and emotions (soul). This may sound absurd but this was the original intent of the Creator. God could have made woman from any part of the male anatomy; nevertheless, the Wisdom of God specifically chose the *rib* of

Adam. Woman is made from a bone that stabilizes the structure of the most important parts of the human body and the rib covers the front, side and back of the body. This is the innate idea of Woman from God. She is not the strongest bone in the body but by far not the weakest either. She is made to have strength and maintain structure, as she is also connected to the spine or sternum she is flexible. The rib is flexible enough to understand priorities of how things should function. She is also strong enough to withstand hard blows. For men the idea that she is a protector, and primarily your protector in marriage, this idea will break down levels of ego that may have been hidden in the heart. Being married to a woman is necessary. Understand that one of woman's important jobs is to protect man from evil. This is why a woman always knows when something is wrong. This unique skill is carried from mom to daughter and from generation to generation. Woman is also made to procreate. She is the gateway to generations. All life flow through her! Another gift that woman has is the ability to see. Women will pay close attention to details. The ability to see is connected with the spirit of discernment. Remember she was his rib, so she was covered by skin from her inception. She sees what is in the dark much clearer than her counterpart. She is also innately gifted to see evil, and enemies. The serpent was the first to speak to her and have her question her role and assignment. The serpent had her to recite the command of the Lord. The command according to scripture was not to eat of the fruit from the tree in the mist of the garden notwithstanding; the serpent added 'you *shall not* surely die'. Though knowing truth and not to partake of eating the fruit; because she had never seen the consequences of disobedience, she questioned if she *would* surely die. This was the beginning of failure for the woman. Inside of questioning God's covenantal commands resides the questioning of significance. When one questions the significance of God's command they also question the significance of His and their existence. This level of questioning happens consistently in the nature of man and woman. No one is exempt of the test of obedience. We all must obey! This doubt inserted by an open-ended question lured Eve into changing her mind about the command. In marriage, the mindset of one individual is not individualized. Marriage unifies you two together indefinitely! Your mind is unified together, your bodies are bonded together, and your hearts are joined together. In reality, together "they" made the decision to eat the forbidden fruit. Together they made the decision to be enticed by its intellect and its government. The serpent made a bold statement to them both and said that "when you eat of the fruit in the midst of the garden, your eyes will be opened, and ye shall be as gods, knowing good and evil." This provocative statement shifted both Adam and Eve's mindset to disobey God furthermore, opened the doors for questioning his leadership. Convinced that they had been in the dark about their existence they decided to explore what they had never known before. Truly this couple had everlasting life. They were in Eden, the place of absolute pleasure. Everything they could ever want was there. Covetousness, ungodly ambition, lust and desires drew them away from the original precept. This happens to many awesome marriages. Curiosity kills the cat. God never intended for us to be *like* gods but to be in *likeness* of the Most High God. The original intention was that we only know good. Not that we know or be intimately acquainted with lies, divination, spells, deception, magic, illegitimate knowledge or an illegitimate government, which is the essence of evil. When one takes part in evil one takes part in sin. Because our minds are invaded with demonic suggestions, it is easy for us to think that the evil we do is good for us. This is the mixture that God never intended us to have.

Healthy Marriages Create Happy Families

Genesis 3:4-6 "And the serpent said unto the woman, Ye shall not surely die. For God doth know that in the day ye eat thereof, then your eyes shall be opened, and ye shall be as gods, knowing good and evil. And when the woman saw that the tree was good for food, and that it was pleasant to the eyes, and a tree desired to make one wise, she took of the fruit thereof, and did eat, and gave also unto her husband with her; and he did eat."
Genesis 3:4-6 KJV

In scripture, the woman saw that the tree was good for food. This legitimate inspection came to her second nature because of her gifts to see. However, after speaking with the serpent Eve's eyes had not seen things the same way that she did previously. She saw as one that worked for another team. When you are working for the wrong team evil looks good for food. Evil looks good to be a part of, ingest, and co-exist with. Evil begins to deceive the eyes. What you saw before is no longer what you are seeing now. Your eyes become instruments of lies. The lies create desires you were never intended to have. Lust will have you wanting more of the very object you already have enough of. Lust and covetousness drives the imagination to murderous levels of ambition. Your desires and ambition was designed for God. God brings solutions to passionate ambitious desires. God is the only One that can fulfill the soul. Neglecting the original intent of Adam and Eve's purpose is the dominant cause of the fall, the loss of identity and sin nature as well as death to be the vein of existence. This is still happening now! In marriage, we often have great intentions; all the same, they are derailed by what is happening on the inside of our souls.

We want all the marriages in the world to prosper especially those that love God. The bible says that you will prosper even as your soul prospers. Most marriages focus in on all the sought-after issues like: communication, sex, and money. Oftentimes neglecting the main issue that governs all three. Our soul will govern how spouses communicate with one another, what you do with your money and how you proceed in your sex lives. But what should govern your souls? The correct answer is ***Jesus Christ***. Jesus is the perfect Government! He gives perfect guidance when you don't have all the answers. God is the source of all relationship. God is the source of healthy marriages. When your soul is governed properly all of the areas of your lives are governed properly. It is paramount to have a relationship with Christ. To have a relationship with Jesus you must be willing to submit your life to Him! **You must submit to his Lordship.** Jesus should begin to take precedence over your entire life. Total submission to the will of Christ is what the Christian walk looks like. Lay down your life of sin nature to gain a life full of abundance and love. God loves you with all of His might, and he demands the same from you. This is where successful relationship and Marriage begins! It begins with learning to love God.

Marriage was created in the Garden of Eden.

Marriage was created in the Garden of Eden. *Eden* is defined as a place of delight. They lived in constant pleasure, delight and overflow. Because Adam and Even both held the ability to walk in the spirit, there was no LAW and everything was fruitful, bountiful and abounded in their direction. This is the same place that Jesus redeemed through the cross. Through the finished work of the cross, Jesus Christ's intention was to redeem the entire of life of the believer. This means your marriages are to return to a state of delight, full of: purpose, destiny and distinction. In addition, living a life of peace and tranquility in the absence of the curse of the fall. For women, the possibility of the sting of childbirth is not a phantom but a reality with the emphasis of your children's presence still crushing the enemy's kingdom. For men, the ground (making money) is not a hardship; the ground [your sphere of influence] will yield to you and your legacy and generations. As married couples, our lives are designed to reflect the glory and splendor of heaven down to the most finite things that we do or create together as a unit!

Family Unit was not created in the garden.

The family unit occurred after they were expelled out of the garden. This is the place of real life, depravity, struggle, hurt, betrayal and wounded hearts.

It is amazing how you can seemingly have this blissful courtship. Everything is fruitful, lovely, and sweet. You stay on the phone until the wee hours of the morning daring one another to get off of the phone, watching the sunrise will we chat and have all the energy to burn the next day and go to work, school and handle every task just to do it again the next day. The chemistry you experience is explosive! You cannot help but to see the one your hearts longs for every day, every minute of every hour. Then it turns serious, proposals happen, weddings of your dreams become reality and now you are newlyweds sparking love and grief everywhere you go. Now it is real. The newlywed fever wears off. (*Which is representative of Eden.*) You each go to work, handle daily responsibilities, paying bills, raising children, trying to maintain a healthy sex life and lastly dealing with each other's flaws. Marriage never looked so unattractive on television and with celebrities. Media can really make marriage appear tantalizing and if you're unmarried society places a stigma on the unmarried lifestyle. Media never truly covers all of the emotional drain and toil that comes along with marriage. Media deals with images, the enemy plays on perceptions. God created humankind, "In His Image after His likeness" and because the enemy is so jealous of humankind he takes the opportunity to plant lies through media (what you see *an image*) on what marriage is supposed to look like minus the image of God in the marital covenant! This is how the Body of Christ and Society gets deceived on the institution of marriage.

Society never gives you an instruction manual on marriage you just do it! The sad part is when you are unprepared the enemy of your souls uses this to his advantage. How? Examine the truth.

The truth of marriage is: two different people, with two different backgrounds, raised two different ways, educated differently, communicated differently are joined together and **must** become **one**! This is a dying process, which is actually good in the eyes of God, but is painful to the flesh of man! Next, you must recognize that (even though the courtship and chemistry was brandished with heat and love and your mate was perfect) you come into the marriage deeply ***flawed*** people! You are marrying their past, present and future! If your spouse had any level of trauma, you are married to that trauma! You are anointed to deal with and destroy this trauma but it is painful when the trauma rises up in the union. As a part of their past you are marrying your mates' **family!** This too can be painful and friction worthy! With busybody relatives and your spouse still feels the need to gain acceptance from family that can wreak havoc in your present.

Present day: you are married to their love language, their sensuality and sexuality which is systemic of your spouse's past, present and future; which can also cause an ailment in your present and future. How? In the event your spouse was taught sex is less than desired, [i.e. "sex is bad" or "Certain sex acts are bad"] chances are the sex drive will be low and needs will go unfulfilled. If your spouse had childhood, teen or adult traumas from sexuality such as: molestation, rape, coarse teasing, insecure of oneself, embarrassed of body size or genitalia, delivered from bi-sexuality or homosexuality to heterosexuality, deep-strange-religious beliefs, high expectations of your sex life and low outcomes with your sex life, pornography (either exposed too young or addiction) chances are these issues will arise and cause disorder within your marriage when the present is knocking on your bedroom door. Understand, the marriage covenant lifestyle is all encompassing! This too deals with past/present woes: money, jobs situations, affections and emotional wellbeing. When either your spouse was raised with a silver spoon in their mouth: expect laziness, selfishness, and spender's mentality. (Remember: ***you*** are equipped to ***destroy*** these patterns in your spouse). Or in the opposite direction, spouse was brought up in poverty: penny pinching, hoarding, self-evolved, strong willed personality type is in effect—in the present day (which ***you*** are anointed to ***destroy*** in your spouse). All of these issues are just a small number to name can cause the enemy to come and put you on a rollercoaster of emotions and seemingly a destructive course to divorce court!

The enemy is **the enemy**! See it just that way. When you first get married couples have difficulties identifying the enemies of their assignment. Sorry, I guess this can be said about all couples, all ages, all cases. It doesn't matter how long you have been married or how great you feel your marriage is. You can have difficulty identifying the enemies of your marriage. Satan has been here much longer than most of humankind, so it is sure that he knows what he is doing. This why I (personally) have seen that one to sixty [1-60] year marriages can end in divorce. When you get married, you are never out of the oven. God is continuously working to make you better. Now lets be clear your assignment is to walk together in love, joy, peace, agreement, perseverance, acceptance, power and authority. You are to walk together until you both pass into the next life with your Lord and Savior Jesus Christ. There is no better joy in life than having your spouse walk with you during the good, the bad, and the ugly times. Now this is really the second most important thing to keep in your mind. It is the fact that indeed you both are walking together a whole lifetime. The operative word is **together**!

Can two walk together, except they be agreed? Amos 3:3 NKJV

So, they are no longer two, but one flesh. Therefore, what God has joined together, let no one separate. Matthew 19:6 KJV

Again, the enemy is the enemy! That means that anything both *natural* and *spiritual* that tries to separate you from your spouse is the enemy. Anything both natural and spiritual, that is not beneficial to you and your spouse is the enemy. **Anything that is, natural or spiritual, that is an enemy to one spouse has now become an enemy to both people in the marriage covenant.** This is extremely important. You have had the wedding of your dreams. You are married to the spouse God has handpicked for you. You love everything about your spouse. You have been soul-bonded. Your marriage has Gods hand on it. You have been blessed beyond your wildest dreams. But if you don't *identify* the enemy, the enemy will destroy your marriage in one argument. You never married to become separated. You never got married to be divorced. If the enemy can confuse any of the spouses into agreement that it (the enemy) is good, the marriage will perish. All enemies are deceptive. The enemies come in looking great and awesome. Typically, the enemy will use the tactic to divide and conquer. First, divide this marriage. Break the bond and everything that ties them together. Here is an instance of what your enemy will say to you [do not allow this to happen] "God never meant for you to feel alone in this marriage!" And he knows that one without the other make the entire unit weak. Satan will also use people to try to divide your marriage. It can be friendships that want too much information; in-laws constantly invading your personal space or the random attracted individual vying for a place and affection in your life. Any person that conveys, infers, has the demeanor of or even gestures the breakup of your marriage is now your enemy. Build big and fortified boundaries. Remember your primary goal is to protect the marriage God has given you. You must protect your marriage from outside invaders. If you have issues then you must protect your marriage from inside invasion as well. You must identify any and all traumatic experiences that has occurred into the marriage with you, i.e., molestation, rape, child abuse, perversion and sexual proclivities, strange views of marriage or expectations of what a spouse is to be based on images (dysfunction). Your marriage has been deemed pure, undefiled and to be honored among all. Marriages are made of individuals that come into covenant that are deeply abused, tortured and minimized. Every person has deep wells attached to their human experience. And all of these wells have emotions attached to them that are detrimental. You may have reoccurring memories that cause pain and depression. You may have had perverse sexual acts happen to you that you now feel are normal. You may still be deeply hurt by your previous relationship. You may be driven by the abandonment of your parents. The enemy uses: thoughts (strongholds), ways of being and lifestyles that you would never indulge in under sober mind--indulge; will walk into the marriage and make its home. Evict these demons, cycles and strongholds out of your marriage! Be bold! Place the bonds of purity back on the top priority of your relationship. Purity comes from the Word. More importantly, purity comes from biblical character being enforced. This will bring normality to your marriage. The Word in action is the new normal. If it is not normal (biblical) kick it out. If you cannot see what is happening within yourself then ask your spouse to be brutally honest with you. Questions such as: "Where am I missing the mark?" and "Tell me the honest truth of your opinion of where I am heading" will assist in achieving self-transformation. Inform your spouse that you want to be better. You may also need counseling to achieve this goal. This is definitely ok. Based on the maturity of both spouses this may be the best option. Do not be afraid of growing your marriage. Having good counseling is one of the best ways for marriages to grow. Be sure to only go to people you both agree with. This does not void out the idea of friends you can talk to, friendships are necessity to healthy individuals and marriages, but indeed putting an emphasis on going to professional counselors that are lead by the Holy Spirit. Why? Because marriage has been sanctioned by God. You need godly people with the spirits of wisdom and counsel in your corner when you deal with deep and hard things. You also need someone that will pray and not gossip about what you are growing into or out of. Someone you can both trust. If one spouse is not in agreement with talking to another it must stop. And stop immediately, it doesn't matter what you feel or what you think. This is called submission. This is respect. Everyone is not allowed to speak into or about your marriage simply because there may be bad intentions. Keep this in mind that there are more people that do not have supernatural ability to build your marriage than those that do. You are the primary builder, protector, and communicator in your marriage. You are first line of defense. You are the husband or wife. You are anointed for your marriage. You were sent to build your marriage. Don't let anyone or anything take your place.

Secrets

Satan will use secrets to try to divide your marriage. Satan will also try to use lies and deception to stabilize the secrets. Secrets are ticking time bombs. They have a timer and eventually the timer will ring and there will be an explosion. Do not allow secrets into your marriage. Stay naked and not ashamed. Your spouse should be the only one to see you totally naked. No secrets. Nothing hidden. Withholding nothing. With God, you are always naked before him, even when you wish you weren't. It is the same in the marriage bed. This means that from the bedroom all the way out to world you must lay everything bare for your spouse to see. This is the original intent from God. Adam and Eve were always naked. They just didn't know it until their eyes were opened to the shame of their decisions. When you are married there is no more shame. Leave that outside the door. Just as in Christianity there is now no condemnation to those who are in Christ Jesus (Romans 8:1 KJV), there is no more shame in marriage. You will never make all the right decisions both of you understand that. There is no reason to lie or conceal secrets. You shouldn't have secrets about your past, your present and future endeavors. Don't let the devil tell you that the other spouse is better off not knowing. Don't let the devil tell you that you can die with this secret: terms like, "take it to the grave" will hinder the peace God wants to give to your marriage. Don't let Satan pervert scripture by saying, "don't let the left hand know what the right hand is doing." If it involves keeping secrets, God is not interested. Satan is the ruler of darkness. He loves ruling your life by keeping things in the dark. Here are some areas that Satan will promote keeping secrets in:

1. *Finances* – This is one of the first areas Satan will attack in marriage. Secret accounts, secret stashes, secret retirement funds, secret business accounts, secret checks, secret credit cards, secret investments, stealing a little bit of the car note every month, or stealing from any of the bills is totally a trust killer and divides marriage. Money is a very personal thing to individuals but when you are married money is to be openly talked about and shared. It is

my recommendation to have all joint accounts. Both spouses should be able to see everything. Deception in money brings division into marriage.

2. *Feelings* – It is amazing how we allow Satan to tell us we cannot express our true feelings to our spouse. This is a lie from the enemy to get you to implode and fail. Satan knows that you were made for sharing so he will insert selfishness, or fear. Selfishness says, "The other person doesn't deserve to know how I feel". Selfishness says, "I need to keep my feelings to myself because they are not strong enough to handle them". Selfishness and fear says, "I'm afraid the other spouse will blow up on me, I cannot tell them anything. Selfishness and fear says, "If I let them in then they will be

able to do whatever they want to me. I have to seal them out". These are all ways the devil has designed secrets to manifest. Do the opposite of what your secret keeping demons tell you to do. Do not keep secrets about how you feel. Your spouse can handle your feelings. They were made to handle your feelings. If you keep your feelings hidden in secret from your spouse how could they ever embrace the real you? You're right! Your spouse will get an imitation version of you. In fact, they won't really get you at all. Because, without your emotions you are not present in marriage. Be present! Be fully expressed. Be authentic, unapologetically who you really are so that you have no doubt that they are in love with all of you. In addition, give your spouse room to react to the real you! Whether your spouse reacts in: anger, shame, sadness, frustration, guilt, happiness, rejoicing, gladness, and appreciation it is all in truth—your truth and their truth. Give them room to be who God created them to be.

3. *Friendly gossip*-This is deadly. When friends gossip about your marriage it is destructive. This happen usually when a secret gets out and amongst friends. Friends that are supposed to be able to keep secrets, have now betrayed you and your spouse. Secrets are devastating at this level because of these three reasons: first, the secret that is out is more than likely an encroachment into the personal space of the marriage; second, now all that have taken part in spreading this secret

are now a part of your marriage bed. (Yes, it is just that intense!); third, if the secret is there it is more than likely something of the embarrassing nature, or something harmful. That means all the friends have something that they gossip about that is not common between all the friends, which nullifies the friendship and ends in broken relationships. Married couples (gossiping) friends create an environment that is not safe. It becomes a pit of vipers. Know that the secret will come to the light and all that knew about it will be held responsible and all that was gained over years may be lost.

4. *Sexuality-* secrets and sexuality can be highly discouraging. When one hides their sexuality, it releases deception into the marriage. One of the spouses

can feel that the other spouse is hiding something. Or sexual secrets can have the propensity to trigger your spouse to feel suspicious. Secrets of this kind are very embarrassing. Sexual secrets are scary and daunting. Shame and fear haunt individuals until the secret is exposed. Sexuality is the sum total of whom you as an individual and the sum total of what your marriage is collectively. Sexuality is tempered with: vulnerability, submission, servitude and humility because of its tender nature (unveiled to the senses of your spouse and God). When sexuality is disguised it causes one of the spouses to not fully embrace or know the other and this shows up as feeling disconnected from your spouse. Sexual issues can look like many different things. For example: sexually deviance, or sexually enraged, desire sadistic play, or lustful, or sexually over stimulated, sexually under stimulated, needy, dysfunctional, all the way to not functional. Sexual sensuality stems from the first concepts and ideals of sexual orientation. Based on an individual's first sexual encounter or habitat they could be subject to sexual perversion. When the intent for sexuality has been twisted it will not perform its purpose. This is the bottom-most level of abuse and ultimately the defiling of your marriage bed. If you or your spouse considers that the outlook on sexual pleasure is perverse both must seek counseling and deliverance. If your secret is that you have been sexually molested, or raped (by opposite sex or same sex) or incest, you must share this secret with your spouse and seek out counseling and deliverance with someone you both trust. It is always best that both spouses go to counseling together in such cases. The purpose for sexuality or having sex is to enjoy and take pleasure in your spouse, procreate, display godly love, restore, heal, bind the family together, as well as worship our living God together. Secrets in sexuality will create problems between the spouses in sexuality and finances. You must seek to have purity in your sexuality. God created you and sex. He knows everything about you as well as the entanglement on how you got to this place. Confess sexual secrets aloud to God denounce them. Sexual secrets are some of the most destructive secrets because they can harbor curses and generational curses. These curses can attack: the body, money, as well as the family. Break these curses and release the blood of Jesus over: your body, your finances, your family, and your generations!

5. *Attraction-* secrets can be menacing to the marriage as well as the marriage bed. When one is secretly attracted to someone or something that is not the other spouse it is the spirit of perversion at work. There can be same-sex attraction, object attraction, inordinate attractions, incest attraction, and many other levels of attraction. Being attracted to what is not ours is covetousness. Attraction will drive sexual appetite. *Attraction is appetite.* Attraction is an open door that

must stay closed in all marriages. Win this door is open it creates: adultery, lust, lewdness, uncleanliness, and fantasy lusts. Ungodly attraction will draw men and women out of their marriages. This drawing or appetite is fueled by desire. When desires are toward the wrong: individuals, things, places and ideas it is likened to herding wild oxen. Because lust is activated false emotions become attached to desires and attraction. When the attraction and attention is not on the spouse and this happens, it is called an affair or pseudo- spouse.

"I tell you that anyone who looks at a woman to lust after her has already committed adultery with her in his heart." Matthew 5:28 KJV

"do not desire her beauty in your heart, nor let her capture you with her eyelids." Proverbs 6:25 KJV

"but each one is tempted by his own evil desires he is lured away and enticed. Then after desire has conceived, it gives birth to sin; and when sin is fully grown, it gives birth to death." James 1:14-15 KJV

If you feel as though you are not attracted to your spouse or less attracted to your spouse or that you are attracted to another person **confess** this sin to God as well as your spouse. Confession will eliminate darkness from your marriage bed. Confession will also eliminate confusion from your marriage bed. Confession brings healing and deliverance to you and your spouse. What you find attractive and not attractive should never be a secret. Married couples should only be attracted to God and own spouse. Ask God to eliminate all other attractions, desires, and lovers. Cut the cord of deception and the lie that binds it. Kick this demonic force out of your marriage bed. Pull out your battle-axes and wage war for your heart and mind. Pull down strong holds that would try to commit the heart into injustice. This evil force will not go down without a fight. It will try to say that you do not have to do all of this. This type of attraction is normal. Do not allow those lies to take root. The Word of God and its truths are the *norm* and the *standard*. After establishing this truth, you must stand on it and begin to direct every desire to the word of God. Return and focus your attractions to the object of your affection. The object of your affection is always God first then your husband or wife next.

6. *Dreams-* Secret dreams are taboo. Most people feel that their dreams are personal and should never be shared. When a spouse has a dream of doing something but conceals it from the other spouse it really hurts. The other spouse is left with thoughts like, "why didn't he/she tell me?" "They don't feel as though I can help?" "Do they feel as though I will sabotage them?" Instead of torturing your spouse with unanswered questions and secrets fill them in to what your dreams are. Your spouse will be highly appreciative and supportive of all that you hold dear. Have no shame in what you dream about. Shame causes secrets. Understand, the

person lying next to you hold the key to all your dreams coming true, but you never tell them. This second half of dreams can be quite embarrassing. Seeing as we do not control what happens while we sleep we are subjected to what is happening in our dream state. Sometimes these dreams can be perverse, unclean, sexual, enticing, wicked, prophetic, or even scary. No matter how weird or crazy the dream is, feel free to give your spouse the dream. This will draw you closer. This will eliminate shame and close doors on demons trying to oppress you in your sleep.

7. *Childhood Drama and Trauma-* these types of secrets are never easy to handle. When someone comes into the marriage with childhood trauma it can definitely wreak havoc. Oft

times traumatic childhood memories are suppressed as a result childhood memories and traumatic events typically spring up from events in marriage. When marriage pressures are at an all-time high, that means God is cleansing and delivering at an all-time high. Marriages grow stronger because of pressure. Because marriage always conducts pressure (power) traumatic experiences from childhood rear their ugly heads. One may start masturbating because as a child he was molested. One may start drinking uncontrollably because of the abandonment of her mother. One may swell up in anger and want to physically abuse the other spouse because as a child they saw their parents physically hit one another. Childhood drama and trauma can be passed down from generation to generation (generational curses) if kept a secret. Demons will say things like, *"what happens in this house stays in this house."* Demons would say, *"Do as I say not as I do."* These statements are antichrist agenda to keep both spouses from reaching full healing and deliverance as well as your god given destiny and potential. If your mind is tipped into frustration because of childhood memories, consider counseling and deliverance. The outraged inner child can swell with outbursts of anger that remind you of *The Incredible Hulk*; this is because your inner child is still fighting for justice as an adult. If your marriage has no peace, always arguing, always on the rocks you can no longer turn a blind eye and keep this a secret. These types of secrets have killed many people. When the pressure of marriage causes reoccurring memories, please do not keep your mouth closed. Instead open your mouth and talk! Talk to your spouse and talk to God. After the secrets have been uncovered you must seek counsel, prayer and deliverance. When you get married you are not only married to the present but you are also married to your spouse's past.

All of the aforementioned secrets are highly detrimental to any relationship or marriage. Let there be no secrets amongst married men and women of God. I must give you fair warning. Tampering with any of the seven high impact *secret* areas may not make your spouse happy. Your spouse may feel as though their individuality is being snatched away. Frustration, anger, and demonic activity can and may follow when secrets are uncovered. You must intentionally build a disciplined prayer life. This is the most important ingredient to all marriages. I know that this is the hard route. It is definitely the long hard route, but it is absolutely essential for any marriage that does not want open door for Satan to walk through. We can cause our marriages to be unbreakable.

Marriage Hopefuls

While single there are a host of questions that come to mind and feelings that can become overwhelming. The feeling of loneliness is a deep pain that only Jesus Christ heals. Many are in hope of a fulfilling marriage. Doing marriage and courting God's way is the proven way to success.

1. *Interested in marriage the first thing you must do is get saved.* What this means is go to church and give your life over to **Jesus Christ**. Accept Jesus as your Lord and Saviour. Begin a fruitful relationship with Him. Your worship life should consist of daily: prayer, worship, reading and studying the Word of God. Steady growth in the character of God will be the result. Doing this will change your life and

ultimately the outcome of every relationship that enters your life. You need God to govern your relationships, but it starts first with a yielded and submitted heart. If you have had relationships based on: abuse, sex, or lust it is more than likely it could not work out. Lust, perversion, sex and abuse (leaving the natural purpose) do not have the strength necessary to feed a long-lasting relationship. Now please do not accept Jesus as lord and Saviour out of compulsion or desperation to gain a man or woman. Do not receive salvation because all the best women/men are in church. Do not do it because it's the only way to get with someone. You must accept Jesus because you know that He is the *Way, Truth, and The Life*. You should accept Jesus because you trust his guidance. You should accept Jesus because you are drawn to his love and compassion. You should accept Jesus because you need him to be a better person. You get saved and accept Jesus because you love Him.

2. *Once you have gotten saved learn to love God.* As a single you will battle a lot of demons, but the demon of loneliness will drive you into the bed or house of another lover. Remember that God is a jealous God. He will have no other Gods or people before Himself in your life. In battling loneliness, you must love God and know the purpose of your life in Him and do just that! When you love God, you put Him first. Learning to do this may take some time. Loving God is worth every second.

You love Him more than your own desires. You make God your first and primary desire. God becomes the object of your affection. The things of God become insatiable. You lay down your self-righteousness and begin to depend on him for all answers. God and the Holy Spirit govern all even what you eat, wear, listen to, or stay around. When you love God not only will you have personal demons that you become more aware of but you also realize that persecution is your middle name. Hard times come but you walk them out with Jesus. You have hard issues you feel like you cannot handle you pray to the Father for strength and wisdom. Seek godly counsel from a wise source. Know this: best friends may leave, family may ostracize you, but you have a friend in Jesus.

This is how it looks to love Jesus: *hard times, good times, terrible times, times of joy, times of utter sadness times of insensitivity, trying times, adventurous times, amazing times and times of happiness.* It mirrors the marriage you will eventually take part in. The difference is when you get married you make room for God in your life. You stay in love with Jesus. Your love for Jesus never goes away nor dwindles. But it remains everlasting and passionate. Just like the love God has for you. What happens is God allows you to create space for a courting situation and ultimately marriage. When you love God, you are a well-balanced individual because God governs your time and heart.

3. *Learn to love yourself.* Because you are in love with God, He will teach you to become a good steward. Loving yourself is the basis of being a good steward over everything God has given you. This is from taking care of your hair to trimming your toenails. God is a God of excellence and care. Because of loving God live your lives reaching to obtain the character of God. The character of God is wrapped in passionate love. His love never leaves His beloved in need. His government dictates that you love yourself just as much as He loves you. You must take care of yourself. Take care of your body. Take care of your possessions. Take care of your career. Take care of your family. Taking care of family is indeed taking care of you. After those things are taken care of

your stewardship goes into the church then the things in your community. Yes, as a member of a church it is entrusted to you (to care for) and your stewardship even though you may not be the lead preacher. God looks at stewardship and love differently. Loving yourself should spread your stewardship from: yourself, to your church home, and overflow into your community. Loving yourself has nothing to do with selfishness! Love is selfless! Just as God is in the condition of Love and establishing His people all the time. The condition of loving yourself will cause you to build your life. If your life has been wrecked do not let it stay there. If you love God and you hope to marry one day. Be sure to ready yourself.

4. *Prayer.* Many marriage hopefuls get to this step and neglect the most important tool in marriage, courtship, and unmarried. Do not forget to pray. In building life and making life reflect the glory and character of God prayer cannot be forgotten. Your prayer life is as important as the heart beating in your chest to sustain life. Without a heartbeat, you cannot live. Prayer is the lifeline of every believer because it is direct fellowship with Jesus. Excite yourself and spirit man with new things. Press your growth in the Lord. Experience new gifts, prayer languages, and areas of service. As you pray and seek the Lord for the perfect will and timing for soon to be spouse, open your vision to God's vision for your marriage. "Is this person in

alignment with the desire of the heart of God for my life?" As you ask these questions and get answers begin writing them down. In fact, as vision opens up write down every attribute impressed on your heart and mind. You will soon have a long list of items. Feel free to add to the list some of your desires that may compliment what God has released. Remember God knows what we need, and knows what is best for us. Trust Him and do not erase the things he has impressed upon you for the things you think are better. His Lordship is best. Our God is a God of liberty so add to this list liberally. List everything you are looking for. From complexion, to height, to weight, to eye color. Open your heart on to this list. Leave no stone unturned. This is God creating vision in you. All marriages that will last must have their foundation rooted from a vision in heaven. Write the vision and make it plain. What is the vision of your marriage? What is God calling for you and your spouse to do together? What is the purpose of getting married? All of these questions should be answered while you are yet unmarried. If you are married already be sure to pray, seek God, and get these answers along with your spouse. When you know the purpose of a thing you will not abuse it—abuse definition in psychology is leaving the original intent. What to do with this long list of attributes, and this beautiful vision God has given you? You pray! You pray over each and everything on the list. Consider this as an everyday prayer list. Praying over the husband or wife you are waiting on, as well as the health and prosperity in the future of your marriage.

5. *Dating*-If by the grace of God, you have your vision, prayer list, have learned to love yourself and God then you are ready to date. If you have not completed steps one through four thoroughly do not date. Do not waste other people's time. Everything in the previous steps is listed to protect you from evil as well as ruin. When you are saved you are not compelled to have sex outside of marriage. Fornication is not an option because you love God and yourself. Saved people are not engaged in all night sexting sessions. The love of God helps saved people to create boundaries as to: how long conversations with potential

mates are had at night, how and when dates will be arranged, how long a dating outing will last and having responsible accountability throughout the dating process. You do not want any evil spoken of them. Loving oneself will put boundaries on even when dates happen, how late dates happen, and what happens at the end of dates. Saved people are not tempted to sleep with someone because you feel it's the sure way to keep them. In fact, sleeping with someone you feel has the potential to be your spouse will ruin the courtship and have devastating effects on the marriage. This goes for men and women. Why would someone buy the cow when they can get milk for free? What you have is invaluable. Your sexuality should be shared with the one you are married to only. Your prayer list will create boundaries. If a person approaches you and they are not what has been revealed to you, or they are not what you have been in prayer for gently remove them from your circle. If they were interested in you they may not be great friends into the future. Their intent may stay in a place of relationship and not friendship. Feel free to release this fish so that they find the one they belong to. Your prayer list helps to realize the quality of person you are looking for. You will refuse desperation when you have prayed hundreds of hours for the one in your vision. There may actually be several people that meet the mark for what you have been in prayer for so, never be desperate and never settle. Ladies and Gentlemen it is highly important for me to say that dating is allowed in the Body of Christ. There are many women that believe there is a knight in shiny armor will gallop into her life, pick her up on the white horse and ride away magically into happily ever after... This is not true! It is a farce. Do not believe this lie. Most great marriages start from two people that take interest in one another and begin dating. Most people date to see if this person is worth spending one hundred years with. If we jumped into marriage with the first thing that looked nice, we would be in a world of trouble. Again, it is ok to date. When married you are only allowed to date the spouse.

6. *Here are black flags in dating.* **Black flags mean kill that**

connection. Emotional abuse, physical abuse, mental abuse, drug abuse, high alcohol intake are all signs of disaster waiting ahead! Potential Mate only wants to date you late at night. Potential Mate you are dating always drives everything to sex. Potential Mate does not care if they break promises made to you. Potential Mate is demeaning in any way. Potential Mate creates arguments all the time. Dating goes wrong if the other person is involved in several other relationships. Marriage is monogamous, dating around denotes a non-committal attitude towards relationships and no, potential mate will not change because you have entered into his/her life—or lie. Dating goes wrong if the other person is mysteriously married. Saved believing unmarrieds do not date married individuals. Do not date people that have these traits.

6. *Courting is the next step.* Courting is very different from dating. Dating is more carefree. When you are dating you are on your best behavior. Cultivating this behavior too long can result in a false sense of the potential spouse. Dating for 5-10 years is a bag of tricks. I believe that every person will know if they think you are marriage material within the first and second year. That is if you are dating infrequently. A lot of people know that they want to marry within three to six months. Now within this time frame he/she will not be able to say he/she knows you like the back of his/her hand but there should be a decent

feeling about proceeding on to the next level or stopping the dating process. Dating so long you resolve to "playing house" is not in the original intent. This behavior is deceptive. It causes the whole relationship to be based on lies because both parties are, "dating and trying to be perfect so they will not lose the other person". Desperation and fear plagues the relationship. Feelings are shaky, on the rocks, and volatile together because you never really know one another. This is not the purpose of dating. The purpose of dating is to see if the suitor has the potential to go into courting and marriage. Courting comes after the dating portion. Courting is for those that have decided that the potential title is now shifted to the most definite. Courting should hardly ever last long. But the scrutiny and inspection process is harder. When you begin courting you both have an agreement that you are heading toward marriage. Proposals are made. You both set a date for marriage that is ways away. Do not just jump into marriage. You ask her father for her hand in marriage. If you are worthy the fathers bless the marriage. With their blessing, you both go to your pastor and let them know that you want to get married. From there your pastor should set up marital counseling. If your pastor does not do marital counseling then you both find a counselor. This is where the introspection and aggressive pruning takes place. Now during this time of courting is where you ask the hard-intruding questions. You ask questions about the lives of the great-grand parents all the way to the current generation. Learn everything you can about the family. Learn everything you can about your soon to be spouse. Be sure to note all red flags. A red flag is something that could be a deal breaker. Figure out if you can tolerate what you see from the family. This is a great time to really take a deep look. Some people say do not worry about family because once you get married you will not have to deal with them. This is not true! Family members will always want to know how you both are doing and be apart of your life. Be sure to pay attention to this area. It will show you what you are in for. Children behave like the parents. If the parents love they may also have a loving relationship with you. If the parents are abusive, beware, because abusive tendencies may rear its head in marriage. Let the counselor or pastor that you both submit to, as an authority, begin to deal with: relationship history, childhood issues, parent issues, abandonment, trust issues, sexual past issues or concerns, commitment issues, deep trauma, rape, and abuse. This is the time for deliverance in both the man and woman's life. Do not allow pride in at this time of courting. Begin to lay bare all secrets, even secret dreams, fetishes, and attractions. If you allow pride in at this time and choose not to come under extreme inspection and introspection, you have willingly chosen to allow enemies to walk into the marriage. These enemies will be of the deadliest type because they are enemies that you chose to keep first of all. Enemies that are concealed on the inside are the deadliest because they camouflage themselves as a natural part of a person's personality or mindset. These deadly enemies do not give up their ground easily. You must fight these out of your mind, heart, and protect your soon to be marriage. Keeping demons active is sabotage. It is like knowing that your best friend is a traitor but keep them around waiting for an opportunity to stab you in the back. Do not do it. Like any predator these inner enemies wait for the time when you cannot defend yourself and then they strike viciously. These inner enemies or demons will not play this game for fun. Rest assured that if you are being honest and forthcoming in this courting season you will reap the best results and have truly meaningful relationship.

If you are honest and forthcoming, laying yourself completely bare, and the other person decides that they are not the one for you, it will hurt. However, this is exactly what you want. You do not want anyone that does not have the capacity to handle all of who you are. If they stop the courting at this point you mourn. But, after the pain you will praise God for revealing it to you. You never want to enter into marriage for 100 hundred years with someone that secretly resents, fears, tolerates, and abhors you. This bond is ripe with insufficiency and lacks the supernatural grace to be in a committed relationship. If they leave you while you are honest and forthcoming then bless God for saving you from a lifetime of hurt and pain. It is fine to stop the relationship any time before marriage. Never feel pushed into marriage or sex. Refuse to feel pressured into eternal covenant. There is nothing in this world worth making this decision without sober thought. Marriage is a lifetime decision. It cannot be taken lightly. Some approach the situation with the idea that if anything goes wrong you can simply divorce. If you have this idea you are in the wrong headspace and you probably should not marry anyone at this time. Never go into marriage with a Plan B. Marriage was made to exist forever. Although cold feet may happen, one should enter into marriage confidently. You need to be confident that this is the right person and that this is the right time. There is nothing ever really wrong with slowing down the timing of marriage. If you feel like you are moving too quickly slow it down. Back the marriage date up. It is OK. The other person should understand this. If they are really for you they will be willing to wait until you are comfortable. This goes for sex while courting as well. You should not have sex while courting. Both partners should have respect for one another and encourage each other to holiness. Fornication is still fornication even if you are a week away from the marriage ceremony. Do not do it. Maintain integrity and godly character. If you have sex before marriage it will open the door for adultery. God created the institution of marriage and salvation; when you receive salvation, you are in covenant with God and His word, when you have sex before marriage you break covenant with your partner and God. This covenant breaking spirit is released into the marriage and adultery happens. If one does not have self-control while courting, when there are times of sickness or perceived lack in the bedroom, adultery will pursue the marriage. In marriage, you will not have sex all the time for all 100 years. Everyone would love it to be this way. Life will have you to prove your love by holding yourself completely and only for that person you are married to. Childbirth will have you to be patient and maintain the fruit of self-control. Sickness and injury will provide you with the opportunity to exercise self-control. It is a part of life. You should not temp one another into lustful desires. You should not pressure your mate into sex. Devils say things like, "if you loved me you would do this." Devils say things like, "lets see if we are really compatible". Devils say things like, "if you cannot do this for me then I will go to someone that will". These are all Devilish statements. Do not fall into the trap of Satan. Satan will use even your soon to be spouse to hurt you. If you both maintain Christian boundaries then waiting for marriage will not be a problem. If the potential mate does not have patience now they very well may not have tons of patience later. Understand these statements are wisdom, principles, and strategy to help detect what is happening when you are head over heels in love. Lust makes you do things that you in retrospect may never have done.

7. After courting comes Marriage. Prepare yourself! This is the season that you automatically enter an institution that is completely governed by the Godhead. Whenever a couple enters into covenantal agreement such as marriage, God automatically steps in. God uses the institution of marriage as a weapon to destroy the works of Satan in everyone's life! Sins, lifestyle and habits are on consistent display. Things that God desires to work out of you,

your spouse becomes frustrated with and attacks it. You both are offended and defensive. This is the Father delivering you both into a holy life style. This is the mystery that Apostle Paul wrote about, "This is a great mystery: but I speak concerning Christ and the church." Ephesians 5:32 KJV. Marriage reveals the authority and love relationship between Jesus and the Church. Jesus desires His bride clean, free from distractions, ailments of the world, afflictions of the past, delivered, healed and freely submitted to Him (without spot, wrinkle or blemish). *"Marriage is designed to make you holy"* Bishop Nathaniel Isaac Ph.D. Would frequently encourage in marriage. Wives will pick and dissect and nag. Husbands will fix, analyze and bring solutions.

Many times, husbands or wives do not desire the focus of the spouse. But, this focus is the sole ministry and heartbeat of the home. God is saying through the mechanisms of spouse, "See that right there, I have been seeing that for ages and I want to clean it out" however, most times spouse on the receiving end will feel aggressed or offended. Learn the touch of your spouse. This is his/her ministry specifically to you. Touch brings identity and reveals identity, touch releases an imprint that only you two will have for one another, no one else can impress upon you physically, emotionally, spiritually, mentally, willfully or wholeheartedly like the one God has appointed into your life to complete an assignment to push you to your God ordained destiny!

Marital Warning

Cheers to the unmarried ***inserts high-five*** and says trust me you are fine please: eat, swallow and reflect on Apostle Paul's statement, "***It is good for them to stay unmarried***"
1 Corinthians 7:8 KJV

And

"*Yet (marrieds) such will have trouble in this life, and I am trying to spare you.*" 1 Corinthians 7:28 KJV

Not to detour any hopefuls just a concession and a warning, because once newlywed life wears off 1-3 years and real-life kicks in here comes Satan and his freaky bag of tricks!

Understand marriage is not a joyride. Every individual is warned in scripture that marriage has troubles in everyday life. Married couples must daily work to understand, love and accept spousal flaws, failure and finesse. Parts that spouse finds most unlovable we are called to overwhelm with love and acceptance. We are also to be our spouse's first: minister, intercessor, counselor, lover, friend, nurse, doctor, healer, deliverer, teacher and sometimes parent. Each of these roles carries the weight of emotional drain and fulfillment as well as sorrow and joy. We learn throughout the course of marriage that this is: emotional, physical, spiritual, mental, will working – work. We pour our lives and ourselves into our spouses and this is why either we will find intense anguish and happiness within the union. It is the most emotionally intense relationship on the planet. Marriage is passionate, it is synonymous of the Passion that Christ feels and has done for us at Calvary. Many unmarried will look forward to marriage with a worldly lens of marriage, hoping that one perfect day; there will be this perfect spouse, met with perfect sex and a happily ever after. Remember: you are marrying a real person, with a real past, has a real future that you are to see or force them into. This is the work of your existence! This is what marriage looks like! Unmarried, this is how you can judge if you are emotionally, mentally and spiritually prepared for marriage:

> *Be subject to one another out of reverence for Christ (the Messiah, the Anointed One).*
> *Wives, be subject (be submissive and adapt yourselves) to your own husbands as [a service] to the Lord.*
> *For the husband is head of the wife as Christ is the Head of the church, Himself the Savior of [His] body.*
> *As the church is subject to Christ, so let wives also be subject in everything to their husbands.*
> *Husbands, love your wives, as Christ loved the church and gave Himself up for her,*
> *So that He might sanctify her, having cleansed her by the washing of water with the Word,*

> *That He might present the church to Himself in glorious splendor, without spot or wrinkle or any such things [that she might be holy and faultless]. Even so husbands should love their wives as [being in a sense] their own bodies. He who loves his own wife loves himself.*
> *For no man ever hated his own flesh, but nourishes and carefully protects and cherishes it, as Christ does the church,*
> *Because we are members (parts) of His body.*
> *For this reason, a man shall leave his father and his mother and shall be joined to his wife, and the two shall become one flesh.*
> *This mystery is very great, but I speak concerning [the relation of] Christ and the church.*
> *However, let each man of you [without exception] love his wife as [being in a sense] his very own self; and let the wife see that she respects and reverences her husband [that she notices him, regards him, honors him, prefers him, venerates, and esteems him; and that she defers to him, praises him, and loves and admires him exceedingly].*
> *Ephesians 5:21-33 Amplified Bible*

If you are not ready to serve your potential spouse and submit to them at all times then you are not ready to get married. Marriage is for the humble. Marriage is for the service oriented. Marriage is for those that want to give their entire life to another person.

Men, as a husband you are charged to: at times, be subject to your wife or one another out of reverence for God and the marital institution. Husbands are called to lead the family under the leadership of heaven to establish godly order within the family unit. This means you are the priest of your home and the king of your family, you lead with heavens authority and without a hardened heart, apathy, laziness, fear, timidity, passivity, aggressiveness, anger or abuse. (Abuse is defined misusing a person absent of its original purpose: cheating, beating, down-talking, aggressive tendencies, [lashing out] withholding emotions, withholding finances, withholding sex are all abuse!) This also means, you are called to be your {potential} wife's greatest apostle, pastor, prophet, evangelist, pastor and teacher in addition to, counselor, intercessor, warrior, healer and deliverer. You are called to mend broken areas of childhood, teen years and adulthood. You must come with **remedies** to pain, disappointment, hurt, answers for life's worst questions, light for deep darkness inside of your wife's life. You cannot come without answers! This means areas of your life are not submitted to Christ and you are dull of hearing! Dull of hearing is not good for marriage! You must be quick to hear, slow to speak.... Meaning *hearing from heaven!* Husbands are also called to love their wives as their own bodies, if you abuse your body sexually with sleeping around, pornography, and alcohol, drugs, prayerlessness and bad company... Again, do not interrupt that woman's greatness with your dysfunctions. You have not actualized loving self yet. This is mate abuse in the making. You must love yourself! When you do love yourself, the next level is ***sacrifice!*** Husbands are called to "love their wives as Christ loved the Church and gave Himself up for her to wash her with the waters of the word, to present her faultless to Himself before the presence of God." This is the essence and job description of sacrifice! You must have the ability to put down your own desires, wants and things you think you may need for the good of your wife. If you see her in anguish-- you sacrifice, if you see her in dismay – you sacrifice, if you see her falling behind in her calling—you sacrifice, but you sacrifice and then you cleanse her so that whatever is ailing her is cleansed: past or present-day issues and she is faultless before you and God. Moreover, you must be emotionally prepared to place your [potential] wife over your *blood* family and create a family and lineage with her. (Momma's boys need not apply!)

Unmarried women, this is how you can gage if you are ready for marriage: emotionally, mentally and spiritually. *"Be subject to one another out of reverence for Christ (the Messiah, the Anointed One). Wives, be subject (be submissive and adapt yourselves) to your own husbands as [a service] to the Lord."* Wives are not subject to only herself and her desires…. You are subject to the desires of your husband's vision. Selfishness cannot be a part of a wife. If you are still more concerned with yourself than submission and adaption you are not yet emotionally or mentally ready to be married. Married women must submit all things to the husband so that the house is on **one accord.** You create the atmosphere in the house by your submissive nature. You become the atmosphere of your husband by way of adaption. You adjust yourself to the lordship of your husband, you must adjust willfully, emotionally, mentally, financially, spiritually and physically. You cannot control the relationship through sex, or think to create a husband through having sex with a boyfriend to lure him into marriage...that is setting a trap. Also, in marriage you must be prepared to adapt sexually without control. You cannot shut out sex to get something that is control, which is Jezebel at work. (Literally preparing for war.) You must also be prepared to serve your own husband for the rest of your life's capability. You will serve him physically through keeping the house and rearing children or taking care of him when he is under-the-weather. You will serve him financially by assisting in the fiscal appropriateness of the vision of your household, you will serve him spiritually by ministering to him through the spirit of wisdom and knowledge, praying for him as his greatest intercessor, giving him wise counsel and advice. You will serve him with your spiritual womb by way of birthing out his visions, dreams and goals. You will serve him by your prophetic ear and giving what you hear from Holy Spirit in the spirit of meekness and humility. Moreover, we have another design to add, The Queen, Prince Lemuel's Mother in Proverbs Chapter 31 instructs her son in the spirit of wisdom of what to look for in a wife:

> *A capable, intelligent, and virtuous woman—who is he who can find her? She is far more precious than jewels and her value is far above rubies or pearls.*
> *The heart of her husband trusts in her confidently and relies on and believes in her securely, so that he has no lack of [honest] gain or need of [dishonest] spoil.*
> *She comforts, encourages, and does him only good as long as there is life within her.*
> *She seeks out wool and flax and works with willing hands [to develop it].*
> *She is like the merchant ships loaded with foodstuffs; she brings her household's food from a far [country].*
> *She rises while it is yet night and gets [spiritual] food for her household and assigns her maids their tasks.*

She considers a [new] field before she buys or accepts it [expanding prudently and not courting neglect of her present duties by assuming other duties]; with her savings [of time and strength] she plants fruitful vines in her vineyard. [S. of Sol. 8:12.]
She girds herself with strength [spiritual, mental, and physical fitness for her God-given task] and makes her arms strong and firm.
She tastes and sees that her gain from work [with and for God] is good; her lamp goes not out, but it burns on continually through the night [of trouble, privation, or sorrow, warning away fear, doubt, and distrust].
She lays her hands to the spindle, and her hands hold the distaff.
She opens her hand to the poor, yes, she reaches out her filled hands to the needy [whether in body, mind, or spirit].
She fears not the snow for her family, for all her household are doubly clothed in scarlet.
She makes for herself coverlets, cushions, and rugs of tapestry. Her clothing is of linen, pure and fine, and of purple [such as that of which the clothing of the priests and the hallowed cloths of the temple were made].
Her husband is known in the [city's] gates, when he sits among the elders of the land.
She makes fine linen garments and leads others to buy them; she delivers to the merchant's girdles [or sashes that free one up for service].
Strength and dignity are her clothing and her position is strong and secure; she rejoices over the future [the latter day or time to come, knowing that she and her family are in readiness for it]!

She opens her mouth in skillful and godly Wisdom, and on her tongue, is the law of kindness [giving counsel and instruction].
She looks well to how things go in her household, and the bread of idleness (gossip, discontent, and self-pity) she will not eat.
Her children rise up and call her blessed (happy, fortunate, and to be envied); and her husband boasts of and praises her, [saying],
Many daughters have done virtuously, nobly, and well [with the strength of character that is steadfast in goodness], but you excel them all.
Charm and grace are deceptive, and beauty is vain [because it is not lasting], but a woman who reverently and worshipfully fears the Lord, she shall be praised!
Give her of the fruit of her hands, and let her own works praise her in the gates [of the city]!
Proverbs 31:10-31 Amplified Bible

The virtuous woman is literally *a wife of valor* in Hebrew, which is defined as the anointing of wifehood. We find that this wife is priceless in her approach to wielding the honor of her home and husband. She is found to be trustworthy of her husband and he is safe with her. She creates safety through godly character, not being emotionally aggressive—he can tell her any and everything safely and his heart can rest that there are not any secrets that either he holds from her so she holds from him because of her trustworthy nature. She creates safety by not hiding things about the children from him, not hiding money from him. She creates no deception within the union. She venerates him, validates him, affirms him and ultimately builds her home with the law of kindness on her tongue. She is not unruly with her mouth. But, she is a builder; she does not pluck him down with what he is not. She is an investor, she uses what is in her hands to create wealth for her home, and she is loaded with talents and gifts and makes full proof of them by creating a fiscally responsible lifestyle. She too, is a leader in her own right with her lifestyle of prayer, fasting, word and worship. She gets food both naturally and spiritually for her home so that she is a vessel they can feast from and she imparts this same wisdom with her associates and friends. She is an investor—a planter, both naturally and spiritually for her home. She sees where there is money to be made and creates more wealth from that vine's; she makes moves spiritually and reaps through her gifts and talents as well! Her *arms* are strong, biblically anytime in the Old Testament the word *arm* was used was in reference to healing, deliverance and salvation! Her physical stature is strong, her emotional stature is strong—but her spiritual well-being is strong, she is a: healer, deliverer and salvation (Jesus) is her solitude and the foundation of her strength. Her faith is firm, not wavering not here today and gone tomorrow, it is not buckled by storms of life, she does not experience a spiritual high and then fall out of the faith, but constant and secure. She is firm in her belief of

Christ and His abilities! And, she is confident in scriptural proof of the outcomes of her prayers, actions and life. She understands the goodness of God and reverences Him in the goodness of the outcomes of her work and knows how to enjoy the fruits of her labor with wisdom and godly character. Just like the *Parable of the Ten Virgins* her candle (light and anointing) does not run out, and she is ever prepared in the Body of Christ to work as well as ward off the tactics of the enemy. She is a woman of tender heart and nature, though remarkably strong there is sensitivity toward the human condition. She prepares her home to weather storms of spiritual and natural magnitudes. Naturally she prepares for bad weather by budgeting, making sure her children and husband as well as herself are ready for winter or rain. Whether that means coats and boots or food and water. In addition, she is a woman that understands her royal and priestly stature. She holds herself with esteem and worth. She is the queen of her kingdom (home) and rules with submission and dignity. Others recognize her around her through the purity, righteousness, holiness and queendom that only come with being humbled by the work of the cross in her life. Her husband is an ambassador and is known in the kingdom of God as well throughout the Earth, her prayers have elevated him into a position where influence and inspiration follows her husband's face and name. As a result, she is a woman that knows how to rule the affairs of her home and she is not a gossip or busybody because she concentrates on the well-being and future outcomes of the family that the Lord has given her. And, an added blessing, her children stand firm to say that she has been an example to them and they bless her. Her legacy follows her through her children, and she will be remembered as one that is: happy, fortunate and to be envied.

All of the aforementioned attributes, allows you to see the labor that goes into real life marriage. Marriage is for adults! Marriage is for the mature and spiritually mature! We can no longer go into marriage with big eyes and false images. Images from media must be destroyed to have a healthy marriage and lifestyle within the marriage. Your heart and will must be postured in humility to serve the way that Christ served in order to get married! Though the Church has been wrecked with: illness, defeat, dysfunction, deception and sin—Jesus was sinless and absorbed her punishment before his Father. He separated Himself to His wife, covered for her and though He did absolutely nothing took her place and gave His life to redeem Hers. He untangled where Adam missed the mark in the fall to produce the proper image of marriage. (*Adam said this woman you gave me, Jesus said, "Here I am send me"*). In the same manner, be prepared to **reproduce this image** within marriage.

This is What Marriage Looks Like

Personally: I had absolutely no idea, nor road maps to determine the reality of marriage. My original thoughts on marriages were sadly ungodly worldviews. Of this I had to repent, because I too missed the beauty and splendor of the gift of God's design of marriage. Marriage is a mechanism that God designed as a system to bring: wholeness, health, companionship but most of all ***holiness***. In marriage, we tend to examine spouses up-close and pay attention to characteristics and flaws that annoy or bother. Complain, fuss and sometimes even argue. However, those same flaws complained in the recesses of the hearts and minds The Father is trying to get something healed and delivered within you. Marriage causes a divine mirror to spring up so that you will examine one and see where we too fall short of the glory of the Father. You must take into account; the very thing that the **one** who sees you each and every day, from every waking moment, sees clearly who you are and loves you enough to confront the ugly parts of you and still love you the same. [Sounds like a hidden mystery of Jesus and the Church.] In addition, though one spouse can be fussing and complaining about a trait that is found to be less-than-desired, The Father is also attempting to gain that particular spouses attention to change and be delivered as well. This is the divine mirror that the Lord is dealing within you. You get to see your spouse's yet at the same time are allowed to see one exactly as is and exactly how heaven sees it. You have the ability throughout the years to become more like Christ through marriage. You learn patience and not tolerance, you learn the grace of God not judgment, you learn peace instead of chaos, and you learn the depths of **love**. Through this divine mirror you get to conform more to the image of Christ. Pride is placed on the altar as you humbly begin to admit that the areas your spouses are addressing is in need of Jesus, as well as when God begins to deal with the complaining spouse, you as well get to conform to the image of Christ in that very same area or even other areas that Christ is attempting to getting our attention to. Often times due to delivery of the complaints (wisdom) we tend to miss out of the healing power of God in attempt to defend your personhood to your spouses. We must, however, keep in mind, *this same individual I have married loves me, wants the best for us, has good intentions towards me and indeed this is something that must be changed and freedom must be obtained*! Once you actualize this truth all of the lies of the enemy that creep in stating that, "*My spouse is* *critical of me"* will cease and Holy Spirit can then lead us in all truth to bring us into deliverance.

Satan's Lies Versus God's Truth

Satan does not create! Satan replicates! God creates! It is important to remind you that God created, sanctioned and ordained marriage. So, with this in mind hone in and begin deception versus truth. When you identify where the enemy has placed lies into your marriage so you can effectively kill them with the truth and move together on one accord.

Satan's freaky bag of tricks:

Lie (1), my spouse always criticizes me, he/she must be my enemy, and he/she is against me.

When this lie happens, it spreads into all areas including distrust and then a tree is growing. **Counteract it** with:

"As a result, we are no longer to be children, tossed here and there by waves and carried about by every wind of doctrine, by the trickery of men, by craftiness in deceitful scheming; but speaking the truth in love, we are to grow up in all aspects into Him who is the head, even Christ, from whom the whole body, being fitted and held together by what every joint supplies, according to the proper working of each individual part, causes the growth of the body for the building up of itself in love." Ephesians 4:14-16 KJV.

Reflect: your spouse is not out to get you! This is the same person that you spent every waking moment while your love was fresh! Were their intentions bad toward you then? Why would spouse's intentions suddenly change toward you to negatively impact the marriage he/she is working hard to build? Marriage is designed to make you better! The mystery of the Bride of Christ and Christ is this to make each other clean, better, healed, whole and progressive. A critical spouse (nagging spouse) is not attempting to hurt you but move you forward in life. He/she may see you stagnant and is coaching you to your next dimension of greatness in life. He/ she is not in the way, they are not heckling you, and he/she is prepping you! This same person is on your side like the sports coach attempting to bring the championship of your future in your grasp! This is **LOVE** and **UNITY!**

Pray this:

Father in the name of Jesus I thank you for supplying me with the best cheerleading coach _____.
Father I thank you that our future and destiny is ahead of us and that you are knitting us together on one accord. Father please permit

sensitivity to one another's needs and emotions to grip our lives forever. Let us season our words with love yet allow truth to reign in our marriage so we can become one and reflect you in everything we do! In Jesus name. Amen.

Begin to really reflect on the goodness your spouse is doing and really thank God wholeheartedly that He placed them in this position to carry out your future together. Be thankful. Appreciate them and show them appreciation. Ask Holy Spirit to give you an idea that will touch the heart and soul of your spouse and obey!

Lie (2) My Spouse is Choosing Everyone and Everything Else Over Me. He/she never spends anytime with me.

When the enemy begins this trick of perception he usually causes it to become a dragon later if it is not caught in conversation and prayer. In conversation with spouse, do not come to them with just a problem or issue bring solutions. The issue is misplaced priority. Being armed with this information, come with a plan of action! Make non-negotiable date days. In these non-negotiable date days, everyone and everything comes second to the relationship. No phone calls, business ventures, school assignments, children (except in emergencies), addressing complaints or arguments. These days are set aside for drawing closer to one another. These days are meant for conversation, sharing dreams, goals, encouragement, restoring hope and future plans. Date nights should be met with prayer and love. Do not allow the enemy any access to these days! What do I mean? Have you ever made a date night with your spouse only for it to end in shambles, with aggression, angst and argument? That is the enemy superimposing his will and agenda into your date night. He has effectively stepped in and took the reins of your date night. The devil is not permitted to encroach upon these evenings. Keep the devil out! When the devil infects the date night with the agenda of hell we have to look at the spiritual reproach that is occurring in the marriage:

Blessings can get hindered! Know that when you are a moment away from a blessing the enemy inserts his agendas to hinder the process. The meaning blessing in Hebrew is: *barak to kneel upon* also it means in English: To be happy, fortunate and to be envied. Meaning you, your spouse and home has been kneeled upon by heaven and as a result you are happy, fortunate and to be envied! You have to be properly postured here on Earth. When heaven is leaning or kneeling in your direction it makes your lifestyle happy, you find fortune everywhere and many will be jealous as a result. However, that is not all! The result of the state of being blessed: "The blessing of the LORD brings wealth, without painful toil for it." Proverbs 10:22 NIV. Blessings add to your wealth and life and you do not have to toil for it! You have to be properly postured here on Earth for the outpour. Be prepared for the jealousy do not be shocked or moved, the best ride-or-die partner is beside you for this journey!

Demonic doors can fly open and now the home is susceptible to demons. The less time spouses have to spend with one another the more time demons have the opportunity to influence each individual within the marriage. The enemy of your soul likes to supplant lies for truth. He will intentionally infer ideas about what spouse is doing to drive a wedge. With this wedge demons have gained entry into the home through negative emotions. When there is anger, strife, bitterness, hurt, wounded hearts and sadness there are a plethora of demons that have entered the soulical realm and home. But, the way the enemy is set up; he does not just want to rule your emotional well-being, he would love to take control of your legacy… children. The enemy then is out for causing children to be intruded upon with rebellion, disorder and dysfunctional behaviors, as well as performing badly in school. The enemies of your soul must be tossed out of the gates of your lives and homes. How do you put demonic forces out? "And he said unto them, this kind can come forth by nothing, but by prayer and fasting." Mark 9:29 King James Version. Come on one accord to fast and pray! Put them out! Next, each place a lie had been planted in the mind, heart or perception replace with the truth.

Pray this:

Father in the name of Jesus, I thank you for putting us together for Your purpose. We thank you that nothing and no one will stand in the way of our purposes together in You. Father we collectively repent for placing others in our union and not making our marriage a priority. Father cause us to come on one accord like never before and place one another on You Kingdom as our number one priority from this day forward. In Jesus Name. Amen.

Commit to the date nights and locking out all distractions on one accord. Learn the art of relaxing in the presence of your spouse. Turn cell phones off, have great conversation, be goofy together and just laugh like the old days.

Reminisce how far you have come together, dream towards the future together. Make infallible goals and enjoy one another's company! Reconnect people!

Lie (3) My spouse's family is crazy and annoying, they do not respect our union.

This is also a trick of the enemy. Once you and your spouse are married, you two become one. "*That is why a man leaves his father and mother and unites with his wife, and they become a new family.*" Genesis 2:24 Net Bible. Which means you no longer are just of your parent's household, you are your own household, your own family. Notwithstanding, you are one and melding both backgrounds of each family into one. Communication styles, ways of life, cleaning habits, cooking habits, eating habits now are one. Each must respect each background because husband's background is now wife's background and wife's background is the husband's. Moreover, you are to cleave onto one another as a family and your family takes precedence over anything or anyone else. Do not allow familiarity to destroy what God is creating based on demonic impressions of past lifestyles and camaraderie. Your affections must be set on the one you are married to. With that your allegiance must be placed on the union. Protect your marriage, prevent infiltration and disrespect of your spouse by standing up for them, standing with them and in extended family settings do not leave your spouse alone by themselves. And, in the event extended family members are talking to you about your spouse, by all means put them respectively in their place, love them, challenge them to love your spouse and move forward!

Pray This:

Father in the name of Jesus, cause my spouse and I to come on one accord. Cause all surrounding us to place honor on our marriage. Father give us wisdom, knowledge and understanding in creating relationships with our extended family members so we all can love and appreciate each other. Father knit (spouse's name) and I closer, deeper and higher on one accord, I rebuke breaches from outside influences in our union now and deal with those that hearts are failing to respect our union, in Jesus Name. Amen.

Remember, those same vows from the beginning of your union: to love, honor and cherish... keeping only to oneself, to pledge fidelity and first priority possession of your spouse.

Protect your union! Correct others in the spirit of meekness and assertiveness that attempt to cause breaches within your marriage. You are now one, and no one else has been assigned to walk with you in life besides your spouse. Do not allow anyone or anything to dishonor your spouse!

Lie (4) I want to be accepted by my spouse's family, I am an outsider.

Whenever there is a space in time where one spouse or another is battling the feelings of being an "outsider" there is the presence of demons of rejection. This is a lethal kingdom. It causes detriment to any and all relationships that mankind holds dear. This spirit is a withdrawing spirit and repelling spirit. A person feels and an experience rejection goes through a cycle of withdraw and then repels those that desire to be close. And, when the spouse complains that they are feeling like an outsider the enemy could have gripped this situation and played upon their perception to place the spirit of rejection into the marriage. This spirals out of control in other areas and looks like feeling lonely in the marriage. When loneliness is an effect in the marriage it is the devil losing distraction away from the purpose of the marriage. All in the attempt to break the covenant and make the marriage feel and seem unbearable. These are tactics of the enemy. You are designed to *leave and cleave* however, we are instructed to *"Show ourselves friendly"* if you desire create community within the family be friendly. Not just tolerable. Once the family is shown to completely reject both spouses must then cleave. But, if there is not an attempt to show friendliness and community, there must be an effort made. Our spouses are called to love us with an unconditional acceptance, not extended family members. Family members must come into alignment with the marriage at a point if they so desire a relationship with their original family member. But, to be in alignment with heaven the families must accept the in-law spouse. If not, they run the risk of being in the way of judgment for attempting to separate what God has placed together. But, there is a way to keep offending family members from judgment. ***Leave and cleave.*** Husbands and wives are called to secure the identity of his/her spouses and extended family members are not to interfere with this security. In the event spouse still feels like an outsider and spouse has made an honest attempt to be friendly, you are then required to cater to the security of your spouse. In addition, also seeking out deliverance to get demons of rejection out of spouse so they can live a whole-healthy life without that spirit in operation. Rejection can crop up in many inopportune areas and so one must cater to the spouse and not the demons. By doing this you can secure your spouse and still get the dysfunction out. Let them know that this spirit is in operation and you desire to see them whole and that in the spirit of meekness and sincerity we will pray in earnest so they will not seek affirmation from outside sources—and family members but security comes from spouse and Jesus Christ.

Pray This:

Father in the name of Jesus, we come to you in repentance for areas that are not submitted to your Lordship that brings security and wholeness. Father we thank you that you will cleanse us today. We take authority over the kingdom of rejection and cast it out of our midst now in Jesus name. We loose the spirit of love and peace over our mind, will, emotions and heart posture now. Father we embrace your love, we embrace the finished work of the cross and we embrace each other with unconditional acceptance. In Jesus Name. Amen.

Practice this level of unconditional love and acceptance. Embrace every part of your spouse: his/her flaws, failures, finesse and successes. Be one another's cheerleaders. In the event they feel dejected from each other's families do not judge your spouse, hear their heart of security to be accepted. Encourage them to be friendly and agreeable with your families. Build relationships. In the event the family is unrelenting have the hard conversations of protection of your marriage. Instruct and inspire everyone about the principles of being one and that no one has the right to stand as an enemy of your family and God. If they do not relent and repent your presence they must now miss!

Lie (5) my spouse works too much, will He/She ever have time for us!

This is the demon of misplaced priorities. This spirit of idolatry is wicked. It will prey on the respected working spouse intentions to provide and protect the family. It is terrible and perverse. The drive to see the family prosper is turned against the working spouse creating poverty in the soul of the family. Idol worship strips the family of its covering and drains it of its power. The working spouse takes on more hours to gain money feeding the ego, and the job that has become their god. The desire to be worshipped comes out in conversations such as, *"I go to work for you and the family."*

This happens because the working spouse feels like he/she is not making enough, that he/she is insufficient, that he/she must prove their worth. This is all a part of the lie. You are not working for the spouse or children; you are a workaholic to satisfy voids. Moreover, the spouse that is at home or works regular hours begin feeling lonely and rejected. They will feel less respect in the union. Feelings of rejection, hurt, and pain set in along with spirits of dejection, regression and poverty. Yes, poverty is attached to working too much. Notice what is happening. When one works too much it destroys the union. It separates the two partners and places the job in between them. Even God took a rest. It is also important to note that God is a jealous God. God made your spouse just like Him so your spouse will have righteous jealousy. This means that they are right to identify and destroy anything that is put unjustly in front of them in priority. *"Thou shalt have no other gods before me."* Exodus 20:3 KJV. This is why when couples are not on one accord with priorities everything that you try to build feels like it is being torn apart by the other spouse. Newsflash! My dear friend it is not the other spouse, it is God that is breaking down everything. God desires complete oneness in marriage. Here is the wisdom to restore a marriage that has been rocked with overworking and idolatry. First, both must acknowledge that the job is killing the marriage, or if something is not done will kill the marriage. Once this is acknowledged both must come together with the new priorities of their marriage. Marriage priorities look like this: God, personal salvation, wife and husband relationship, family nucleus including children, church family, extended family, vocation, then all other things like exercising, and extra-activities. God does not place anything ahead of the husband and wife besides worship and the relationship they both have with Him. These priorities must be on the forefront of your mind. The working spouse slows down on gaining extra hours or they begin the search for a new vocation. The spouse that is not working or keeping boundary working hours keeps patience in their heart and encourages the formally overworking spouse. This change is not easy but you can do it with prayer.

Pray this: Lord we come before your throne in humble repentance. We know that we have sinned in your sight. Please forgive us of idolatry. Your word says we will place no other God in front of you. We nullify this evil covenant we have made. We place the blood of Jesus over it now.

We thank you that we are now no longer condemned, and all curses are broken. We choose this day that you are the head of our lives and union. What God has put together let no man or thing put asunder. We stand together to evict all other lovers, and gods out of our relationship. Let your will be done in our union. In Jesus name. Amen.

Lie (6) My spouse spends too much money, I cannot trust them.

In marriage, you must understand the need for balance. Usually there is a spender and a saver that have married. Both tend to disagree on the angle that they want the monies to go. But, you must have an understanding on money! Money is a current; it constantly flows in and out. With this understanding, there must be a plan and a budget in place. We must Budget: Tithes, Offerings, Special Gifts, Bills, Savings, Trips,

Food, Family Activities, Emergencies and Fun. [Fun can be play money or shopping money.] We also, must have a self-payment system for things and activities to make: oneself, your spouse and children feel esteemed. In addition, both spouses have to come into agreement with where the monies are being spent. Before spending, both spouses must be on **one accord.** With the spirit of agreement in monies you push the enemy out of your monies, finances and credit. Pushing the enemy out of your currency you have the ability to hold and retain more monies. Furthermore, both husband and wife must come in agreement on who is better at paying bills **on time** and who is better at **monetary retention.** Both spouses should make plans with the monies long before paydays, on one accord, with each spouse playing their specific agreed upon roles on the days necessary! Moreover, make a vision for the year written out at the beginning of the year on what the family will achieve together as a unit monetarily and what the monies will be spent on, both spouses at this point will have the ability to see, agree and achieve the vision that has been set forth at the beginning of each year. As you both understand your positions in truth as either the spender or the saver, you can function in accordance with your roles and understand your purpose in the marriage. Additionally, in understanding your roles in the marriage you will also begin to grow trust and establish monetary fidelity. Remember: when you sew deception in marriage, in example: hiding money, keeping a stash just in case he/she acts up, going shopping and buying items and hiding them without agreement on the purchases, having separate bank accounts, hiding bank statements and giving money away without prior conversations...you reap the rewards of deception in other areas: trust, infidelity, spouse begins lying, sex life suffers and the blessings of the Lord lifts off of your house.

Pray This:

Father in the name of Jesus, we thank you for establishing holiness, truth, trust, justice and love as the foundation of our marriage. We repent of deception, control, anger, apathy, immature money habits, misappropriating family monies and discord. We ask Holy Spirit to intervene and teach us how to maintain, retain and spend our monies. Give us wisdom daily with our: money, finances and credit. In Jesus Name. Amen.

Now take the time to draw up a family vision for the year. Create a vision board. Discuss, dream, plan and implement structure on what the family of_____ will do with their monies for the year. Take the time to make a plan of action to achieve the monetary plans. Bless one another by creating a budget and a plan with room to give each other grace for their monetary stance. Do monthly checks on where you are heading and making sure you are moving in accordance to the family vision. Repent when failure occurs and show grace when necessary.

Lie (7) We were clearly not meant to be, I guess this was not meant to last forever.

First, God ordains marriage. Second, God hates divorce. We in the Body of Christ must soften our hearts to the heart of the Father. No longer can the Body of Christ cheapen the institution of marriage based on emotions. Emotions must be sanctified in order to be stable and unmovable by circumstances. In marriage, you cannot be circumstance driven. You must be heavenly minded. This teaches each spouse the fruit of the spirit *self-control* and *faith*. You learn not to operate in the now but into the future. However, when you are carnally minded you are circumstance driven. Carnal is being a believer that is operating at a fleshly driven arena. God hates when the Body of Christ operates out of a carnal mindset!

"For to be carnally minded is death, but to be spiritually minded is life and peace. Because the carnal mind is enmity against God; for it is not subject to the law of God, nor indeed can be. So then, those who are in the flesh cannot please God." Romans 8:6-8 New King James Version.

When inference is made that, "this marriage is a mistake and not meant to last forever" you infer that God did not know what He was doing when he joined you together. Circumstances come and go to build your character and to fasten your faith. You experience emotional highs and lows to let you know the Body of Christ needs to press into the Presence of God. Your humanity is supposed to keep you humble. It reassures us that you are in need of Jesus and your spouse. When you infer that God made a mistake with this marriage, you are in **Pride**. You refuse to acknowledge God and at the same time your spouse takes a hit because you refuse to acknowledge he/she. When you refuse to acknowledge your spouses you inadvertently freeze them out emotionally and withhold precious vulnerability from them. In marriage, you are designed to shed self and out inhibitions and be naked—physically, emotionally, spiritually, mentally, willfully, and with fullness of heart. You are to lay all things bare before God and our spouses and be exposed without fear. This is where you experience the Love of God manifest through your spouses. When you are vulnerable you can "let our hair down" and just be authentic. You can be transparent about your whole total selves and not be afraid of ramifications. You can say what really is bothering, scaring, hurting, wounding, angering, irritating, burning within. In addition, you can freely give to your spouse and in return spouse can give to you: ministry, hope, unconditional, safety and love in return. Voids can be filled in the place of vulnerability. You can share your happiness, joys, triumphs, laughs, memories and promotions and in return your spouse can give to you: support, hi-fives, congratulations, ideas, celebrations, surprises, rewards and ministry. This is what makes marriages last, the ability to be exposed and naked. When you withhold your emotions, show frustrations, treat your spouse as if he/she do not matter and are circumstance driven you miss out on the beauty and blessings within marriage.

You are called to cherish the marriage that God has given you. In cherishing it, you keep it sacred. Whenever you keep something sacred you do not entertain negative thoughts about the item you hold dear. You are not supposed to think negatively about your marriages. And, in doing this you proverbially cover up (Just like our predecessors) and put on your clothes. You negate being naked and unashamed. Whenever the enemy supplants the marriages with lies and deception in the matter of *"we are not meant to be*" he is literally dangling a "better life" in our faces to say, God made a mistake with your life. Nevertheless, it starts with a thought. A negative thought. A carnal thought. You do not take the position to tell God, "Not this spouse you gave me, give me another one." You must recalibrate and renew your minds to think the best of your relationships that God had in mind from the foundations of the world to establish a kingdom purpose within the earth!

Pray This:

Father in the name of Jesus, we thank You God for being wise in all Creation and we delight in Your infinite wisdom. We repent for our pride, carnality and illegal wisdom. We renew our minds and reset our thoughts as it concerns our marriages. We repent for allowing the enemy to seep into our mental faculties. We repent for thinking that we knew more than the Father concerning our lives and destiny. We pull down strongholds now of illegal knowledge of our destiny that attempted to supersede the mind of God and these strongholds must become captive to the knowledge of Christ. We loose judgment against Leviathan now in Jesus name according to Isaiah 27:1 In that day the LORD with his sore and great and strong sword shall punish leviathan the piercing serpent, even leviathan that crooked serpent; and he shall slay the dragon that is in the sea. We cut off communication between Leviathan and our mindsets and marriage now in Jesus Name. Amen.

Now that penitence has gone forth, the act of repentance shall begin to work. Negate every time the thought comes to destroy or try your thought life of your marriage. Reset every area of your life where you can identify that you have clothed yourself to keep from being fully exposed in marriage. Begin to reduce your pride (humble yourself) and be vulnerable. Bring all the cards to the table. Lie out every issue of your heart and give your spouse the ability and permission to minister to those areas. Learn your spouse's touch and their identity to your life. Allow them to imprint those areas the way that only they can. Grow up together just this way.

Lie (8) My spouse must not find me attractive anymore; I do not look like what I did when we first got together.

I believe this is a demonic fear and entrapment that the enemy sets up throughout the course of marriage. Courtships start by looking like poster ad models. Then the happy newlywed weight happens. Then the children come. In between all of this time, you eat and celebrate every high moment. Women must learn to love and embrace every inch of your mommy body. Too much inference on bodily appearance is a trick from hell! Men and women must mature their mind and eyes. Do not allow the object of your affection to be shifted away because of: lust, covetousness, and inordinate desires. Mature men must learn to minister to his wife in this area of insecurity and reassure her of the beauty that is your wife. However, wives keep this secret in mind: men are attracted by what they *see.* When the enemy plays upon your insecurities and cause you not to love your bodies you tend to cover up, turn the lights off during love making, use candles to shield and hide versus allowing our husbands to see you as you are the effect is: the holiness, freshness and object-of-affections can shift. When this occurs, it has the propensity of opening up doors for division. You must keep the enemy out of our sex lives, when he gets hold to your sex life in marriage symptoms include: control, manipulation, sterility, withholding, impotence, perversion, pornography, masturbation and adultery. Furthermore, when you dislike our bodies you dislike self. You are actively in iniquity, and it hinders your marriage, because it hinders your love walk. You cannot love others if we do not love self. You are commanded to love others as self: essentially meaning, you must have a healthy relationship with self.

You must deal in the spirit of love and minister to the insecurity and fear and fill the need of security. If you did not know, *you are supposed to make your spouse feel secure.* Bring reassurance, use your words, tell them, "There is no one more beautiful" or "I do not see or desire anyone else" or "I am addicted to you" These words will settle your spouse. Every individual should feel at peace, at home and desired. This settling force will actually aid in having a whole husband and wife and the home force will be so much at peace. In addition, having a secure spouse kicks the devil out of your bedroom and he/she will feel comfortable enough to lose inhibitions sexually. The result of having a spouse that is secure with his/her outward appearance.... **You will have the best sex of your life.** Make your spouse feel secure today!

Pray This:

Father in the name of Jesus, we thank You that we are created in Your image and after Your likeness. Father we repent for not respecting our image. We pull down images and strongholds of insecurity, low self-esteem, low self-image and low self-worth. We bind, cast out and take authority over the kingdom of fear. We loose love and faith now in Jesus Name. Father knit us together and cause us to view each other and ourselves through the lenses of love. Father cause us to come in contact with, encounter and have a revelation of Your Love for us. In turn, let us love ourselves and express this love outwardly to all of Your people. In Jesus Name. Amen

This is the beginning of a beautiful journey! You will experience the Love of God through your spouse and recognize His love in manifold ways in others around you. Let His love engulfs, rapture and surround you. Take this love inwardly love yourself. Love on yourself. Feel and embrace this love by doing simple things for yourself. Enjoy the simplest things such as eating, bathing and hobbies. Then take this love outwardly and love your spouse by doing random acts of love and kindness. Give them compliments; go out of your way for them. Tell them how you love them and show them sexually. Do this perpetually and watch God move into your marriage in new and fresh ways!

Lie (9) I blame my spouse for our failures in life.

When you blame your spouse, you have ascertained the same sin of our predecessors Adam and Eve. Adam blamed Eve for his failure in leadership. God dealt with both spouses appropriately. Husbands and wives both tend to push blame onto opposite spouse when you feel emotionally that you are failing in life. Instead of diagnosing where you went wrong, you shove the blame, argue about it, make egregious statements and sit stewing in your feelings. However, this is not what God desires for kingdom marriages. He desires you to live on one accord and though there may be disagreements, still oneness is what God is after. When you blame your spouse, you bring about the discord and offense. It hurts your spouses when you accuse your spouses for your outcomes it is essentially saying, "You are the worst parts of me" no one wants to hear or feel that rejection from their spouse! Additionally, blame is a demon that once that door is opened, it is a continuum. It is pushed around perpetually. Anytime there is a character flaw or leadership failure or bad business moves, blame will be pushed around over and over causing a bad cycle until God steps in and judges it. You do not want God to step in and judge each individual in the marriage. In examining scripture and you see where: first, Adam blamed Eve for his leadership failure, "This woman **You** gave me did this and I ate" and then blame was pushed by Eve onto the serpent for her end of receiving deception, "I saw the snake and he tricked me and I ate" versus taking personal responsibility of failure. If they had been straightforward with their failures and sins, instead of hiding and blaming God possibly would have rendered another route. However, because they did not seek God out, sunk into shame and hiding and condemnation, that is where they initially missed the mark. They thought by pushing the blame for their failures and sins, God would have forgone judgment. But, God dealt and judged each individual for his or her personal role in the failure. You must acknowledge truthfully our flaws and failures in our personhood. Amid, acknowledging give Holy Spirit permission to develop and deal with our character and restructure your soulical realm to get to a place where you understand true success. Success is promised to you in scripture but you must follow in scriptural integrity to receive it. Succinctly, events of failure must happen so you can learn proper routes to success with the proper soulical posture, as an individual and as a married unit. You must commit our way to the Lord on one accord to receive the breakthroughs, promotions and blessings that come from above!

Pray This:

Father in the name of Jesus, we thank You for being a Good Father who gives good gifts. We acknowledge that promotions do not come from the east or west—horizontally from man, but vertically from you to us. We repent for trusting in things that will fade for elevation and promotion, but we renew our minds to trust You only. We pull down false idols and images of success and cast them out now! We secure success from heaven's view now. We decree that we shall follow Your Precepts Lord and will be obedient to Your Word to eat the good of the land this day and forevermore. In Jesus Name. Amen.

Lie (10) We cannot communicate properly every time we communicate we argue.

The enemy of our souls loves to reside in communication. His first attempt to thwart the plan of God was to miscommunicate the spoken commandment of God. Everywhere in scripture where the enemy appears notice he is always twisting words and scriptural conversations. This is called **divination** twisting, lying and supplanting conversation is a level of divination that Satan loves to use in conversation. In addition, the enemy also uses Leviathan to break down communication. Have you ever had a conversation and you thought your spouse say something offensive and you ask them to repeat it, and they're like, "I did not say that." Guess what?! Leviathan has presented his old sea monster ways. Firstly, Leviathan is a marine creature, which means he lives and breathes through waters. Waters represent life, vegetation, quench thirst...moreover, all things worship and Holy Spirit. Leviathan likes to stagnate life, the flow of Holy Spirit in your lives. How does he do that? Through communication! He will supplant lies in conversations with your spouse; you can misunderstand things, mishear things and argue issues. Furthermore, Leviathan would like to stagnate your worship life, prayer life and communications between Holy Spirit and your spirit. What is his access point? **Pride.** Pride breaks down your sensitivity and humility. Pride hardens your person and your heart. Pride makes us hard-of-hearing. Pride stacks up on your egos and causes an inflated self-view and creates impenetrable walls to your mentality, hearts, emotions and will. This is where arguments and unforgiveness originate. [Some miscommunications and conflict are healthy, so long as solutions come about. When you have conflict without solutions it is pointless.] You must be mindful to keep the enemy out of your communication! Do this by being consistently in the state of humility, meekness and grace. In addition, being merciful in conversation by listening fully without defense, cutting your spouse off in mid-conversation, rant or complaint. Also, when necessary apologize in the heart of sincerity and being kindhearted. In like manner, you must be your spouse's safe place conversationally. The spirit of Pride makes you hard to talk to: pride creates explosive domineering tempers. No one feels safe conversing with an individual that is emotionally unstable. This makes your spouse want to lie and hide versus stand and tell the truth. Pride must be killed in order for arguments to cease and desist. Seek to find out what is really ailing your spouse without anger and offense. Take the time to listen to their heart and be a healer. Take the time to ask questions if you have misheard something or if it sounded like your spouse has said something offensive, give them a chance to give an account for the statement. Give your spouse the room to be him/herself and express him or herself the way they desire. Allow your spouse to tell his/her truth the way they perceive and make adjustments from this point in the spirit of humility and restoration. I assure you, the more you seek to understand and heal the less the conversations will end in arguments and discord. In return, you will receive love, appreciation and alignment with the spouse God has given you!

Pray This:

Father in the name of Jesus, we thank you for loosing your Holy Spirit in the Earth as the spirit of truth. We repent for being: proud, arrogant, unwilling, inflexible and unsafe. We take authority over the spirit of Leviathan and loose the judgment against it according to Isaiah 27:1 "In that day the LORD with his sore and great and strong sword shall punish leviathan the piercing serpent, even leviathan that crooked serpent; and he shall slay the dragon that [is] in the sea." I rebuke now the spirit of strife in my house and loose the fruit of peace now. Father deal with every area inside of both of us that breaks down our communication and cause us to engage each other in the spirit of humility, meekness, grace, love and peace. In Jesus Name. Amen.

Presently, take the time to kill areas of bad communication and demon communication in your home. Listen to your spouse. Ask your spouse questions. Before you make complaints warn your spouse of hard conversations forthcoming. Build your spouse with light conversations and see how you both receive each other from that day forward!

Lie (11) My spouse is lazy and does not contribute anything to the family.

You must cause your minds to understand that there will be times when our spouse will let us down with the caretaking of the house. There will be times of grace and times of hard conversations of unmet expectations of why the responsibility of the house seemingly is solely being shouldered by one spouse. But, you must also seek out why the spouse has cut off care to the house they vowed to build and care for. Is your spouse secretly: depressed, overwhelmed, tired, stopped caring, entertaining the wrong hobbies, being a workaholic, just selfish, has taken up dangerous addictions or affections? At which point, the spouse whom has taken up an extended off time from the house must give an honest account of what is truly going on inside of them to forsake the building, cleaning and caring for the house that they have vowed to build. Spouse that is making the accusations must be prepared to devour the honest response of their spouse. Most of the time the reasons a spouse "takes time off" will be painful for the other spouse to hear and digest. This is still not the situation to make the environment unsafe with instability but with comfort. Then the next issue will be to make a plan to bring the spouse back into the house emotionally and mentally as well as physically; in order to keep chores of the house for most men and women it pulls on each person mentally, emotionally and physically. Make plans and agreements to make the upkeep of the home less overwhelming until both spouses have both equally entered back into the home fully to maintain and upkeep the home that you both vow to keep and maintain. In addition, minister to the ailing spouses needs and bring restoration from depression, fears, anxiety and feeling overwhelmed. In this situation, your spouse needs your touch to assist in mending the ailment. You are more than able and equip to handle the issues that are plaguing your spouse.

Pray This:

Father in the name of Jesus, we thank you for being at the center of our lives and home. Father we invite you into our home; we invite your truth, your ways and your love into our environment. We repent for selfishness and refusing to build the home you have given us charge over. We bind selfishness and cast it out now, we bind and cast out depression and feeling overwhelmed in Jesus name. We loose love, joy and peace into our home now in Jesus name. Amen.

Lie (12) My spouse is controlling; I cannot have any privacy nor any individuality.

This is a complaint that many shares when couples misunderstand the union and commitment of marriage. **There is no individuality in the institution of marriage.** Once your names are both on the marriage license and the minister or judge has married you—you are one. Period. You are no longer two different people but two people who have become one complete vessel. You cannot control an extra individual but you do control your personal outcomes and behaviors. In essence, your spouse is keeping your outcomes and behaviors as a sole unit. Spouses are not controlling: cellphones, friendships (opposite sex or same sex), what you are watching on television, places you visit, foods you eat, the careers that you work. Your spouse is protecting the interest and investment of your home. The interest and investment of the home is the livelihood, wellbeing and longevity of the spouse. All desire and hope for a long, joyful and healthy life with the spouse. Therefore, you must understand that the complaining spouse is not out to control or harm you but to love you and protect your home, lifestyle and integrity. With your spouse, there are not any secrets. What does that mean? In protecting your integrity your spouse should have the lock code on your cellular devices (cell phones, laptops, computers and tablets). Why be offended for your spouse to view your cellular device unless there is something to hide? When you are married there is no longer any "mine" or "yours" it is "ours" in the courts, law call "ours", "community property" meaning it is collectively the families property. In such manner, there is no longer an individual and individual property; you are now one vessel, all property belongs to that one vessel (you both as a unit). Your spouse deserves the right to look at your devices and property (emails, text messages, call logs, social media accounts) because it is theirs as well. We must *submit one to another* in all things even in our property and goods. *Submitting one to another* means: emotionally submitting, physically submitting in body and in goods, spiritually submitting, financial submitting, heart posture submitting, willfully submitting and mentally submitting. When you submit yourselves to each other in all things, God is now glorified and you reflect the image of Jesus and the Bride. You become a living epistle of pleasure to the kingdom of God and passerby's who watch your marriage from afar. Your testimony will begin to fuel others on the love of God and goodness of the institution of marriage. You become restorers in the Kingdom of God by your testimony of oneness. This reveals how: The Father, Son and Holy Spirit are one without division sharing access throughout one another in all equality without one being subversive to one another.

Pray This:

Father in the name of Jesus, we thank you for your sovereignty and Your plans toward us. We repent of individuality and refusing to submit to one another. We repent for placing boundaries on areas that we desire to keep secret. We ask that Holy Spirit take primary position in our marriage and bring: truth, healing, deliverance and health to us both. We take authority over spirits of perversion and deception; we loose truth and revelation over us now in Jesus Name. Amen.

Lie (13) My spouse will never get saved, I quit hoping for their salvation

This is a lie directly from the enemy! At the very base of this lie is a *demonic force* called **doubt.** Doubt locks into your fears and motives, blinds you from the truth of Holy

Spirit and dulls your sensitivity to hearing, feeling and recognizing what God is saying and doing in your now. You must be courageous and have limitless faith and love to allow Holy Spirit space to move in your home and in the life of your spouse. You must keep in mind the principle of love and faith. "The Lord hath appeared of old unto me, saying, Yea, I have loved thee with an everlasting love: therefore, with *lovingkindness* have I drawn thee." Jeremiah 31:3 King James Version. Holy Spirit is the power on the earth that convicts the world of sin. However, Holy Spirit draws people into the salvation and the kingdom of God by way of love and compassion. Holy Spirit does not draw by way of condemnation, condemning behaviors, in example: judging, hateful, rude, abrasive, religious, watchful, nagging, mean, discontent, argumentative, disagreeable and stern. These behaviors **will not** win your spouse that will push them away and have them judge the Savior you serve: ***Jesus.*** It will take more than just prayers and spiritual warfare to win your spouse to Christ but works:

What does it profit, my brethren, if someone says he has faith but does not have works? Can faith save him? If a brother or sister is naked and destitute of daily food, and one of you says to them, "Depart in peace, be warmed and filled," but you do not give them the things which are needed for the body, what does it profit? Thus, also faith by itself, if it does not have works, is dead. But someone will say, "You have faith, and I have works." Show me your faith without your works, and I will show you my faith by my works. You believe that there is one God. You do well. Even the demons believe—and tremble! But do you want to know, O foolish man, that faith without works is dead? Was not Abraham our father justified by works when he offered Isaac his son on the altar? Do you see that faith was working together with his works, and by works faith was made perfect? And the Scripture was fulfilled which says, "Abraham believed God, and it was accounted to him for righteousness." And he was called the friend of God. You see then that a man is justified by works, and not by faith only. James 2:15-24 King James Version

As you see it takes more than just saying that you believe but you must role up your proverbial sleeves and work. There will be emotional work, physical work, mental work, spiritual work, willful work and heart posture work. Your character must begin to also speak louder than your words and become your integrity when words fail.

> *Likewise, ye wives, be in subjection to your own husbands; that, if any obey not the word, they also may without the word be won by the conversation of the wives;*
> *While they behold your chaste conversation coupled with fear. Whose adorning let it not be that outward adorning of plaiting the hair, and of wearing of gold, or of putting on of apparel; But let it be the hidden man of the heart, in that which is not corruptible, even the ornament of a meek and quiet spirit, which is in the sight of God of great price. For after this manner in the old time the holy women also, who trusted in God, adorned themselves, being in subjection unto their own husbands: Even as Sara obeyed Abraham, calling him lord: whose daughters ye are, as long as ye do well, and are not afraid with any amazement. Likewise, ye husbands, dwell with them according to knowledge, giving honour unto the wife, as unto the weaker vessel, and as being heirs together of the grace of life; that your*

prayers be not hindered. Finally, be ye all of one mind, having compassion one of another, love as brethren, be pitiful, be courteous: Not rendering evil for evil, or railing for railing: but contrariwise blessing; knowing that ye are thereunto called, that ye should inherit a blessing. For he that will love life, and see good days, let him refrain his tongue from evil, and his lips that they speak no guile: Let him eschew evil, and do good; let him seek peace, and ensue it. For the eyes of the Lord are over the righteous, and his ears are open unto their prayers: but the face of the Lord is against them that do evil. And who is he that will harm you, if ye be followers of that which is good? But and if ye suffer for righteousness' sake, happy are ye: and be not afraid of their terror, neither be troubled; But sanctify the Lord God in your hearts: and be ready always to give an answer to every man that asketh you a reason of the hope that is in you with meekness and fear: Having a good conscience; that, whereas they speak evil of you, as of evildoers, they may be ashamed that falsely accuse your good conversation in Christ. For it is better, if the will of God be so, that ye suffer for well doing, than for evil doing. For Christ, also hath once suffered for sins, the just for the unjust, that he might bring us to God, being put to death in the flesh, but quickened by the Spirit: By which also he went and preached unto the spirits in prison; Which sometime were disobedient, when once the longsuffering of God waited in the days of Noah, while the ark was a preparing, wherein few, that is, eight souls were saved by water.
The like figure whereunto even baptism doth also now save us (not the putting away of the filth of

> *the flesh, but the answer of a good conscience toward God,) by the resurrection of Jesus Christ: Who is gone into heaven, and is on the right hand of God; angels and authorities and powers being made subject unto him. 1 Peter Chapter 3 King James Version*

I Peter Chapter 3, imparts specific character landmarks to live by in order to draw an unsaved spouse into the fold. Saved husbands and wives gain a greater knowledge to do a greater self-introspection on how your behavior is affecting your spouse that is waiting to be introduced to a real Jesus. Firstly, for wives that husbands that **do not obey the Word** your behaviors and must still read respect, honor and subjection. Just because Husband is not saved does not give you the divine right to disrespect your husband! You still must defer, ask for his opinion and be pleasant to him. Additionally, Apostle Peter reveals the inward beauty is to be met with: meekness, holiness, peaceful spirit, humility and graceful. Then Apostle Peter gives us a point of reference, Sarah. Sarah had endured a lot of traumatic hardship, emotionally as the wife of Abraham. Out of fear, Abraham allowed another man to marry her; infertility, the pain and doubt of infertility gave way to her allowing Abraham to lie with Hagar, the servant girl and producing an illegitimate heir. Notwithstanding, Abraham chose to lie with Hagar (he did not have to he could have reassured Sarah's faith), this is why Sarah says to Abraham is recorded saying to Abraham, *"Then Sarai said to Abram, "My wrong be upon you! I gave my maid into your embrace; and when she saw that she had conceived, I became despised in her eyes. The Lord judge between you and me."* Genesis 16:5

New King James Version. Which means, there was a marital woe of the feeling of betrayal. She did not judge Abraham she allowed God to deal with him; Sarah judging Abraham had the propensity to separate Abraham from the promises of God and had Abraham living out curses. The graceful posture that Sarah held kept the promises of God over them and their perpetual legacy. Accordingly, you are daughters of Sarah so the legacy to win your spouses with godly character is in your blood! You have the divine rights to have saved husbands and children! Likewise, husbands you must handle your wife according to the knowledge of God that you have. In this scripture, it can be misread to believe that you are handling your wife with the knowledge you have of her. This is contrary, if you handle your wife according to the knowledge you have of her fleshly character it only ensues bondage and fleshly behaviors to grow. "However, if you handle your wife according to your revelation of God"—Apostle

Terrence Malone, then you will receive the foresight to see exactly what it will take to cause salvation to spring forward. An added benefit in handling your wife in accordance to your knowledge of God, you understand her role and sin nature, but your prayers will not be hindered!!! Your right as an heir and ambassador of the kingdom of heaven is that your wife and children are saved! In addition: *"For the unbelieving husband is sanctified by the wife, and the unbelieving wife is sanctified by the husband: else were your children unclean; but now are they holy."* 1 Corinthians 7:14 KJV, Apostle Paul gives us revelatory wisdom and spiritual edge that your spouse has already undergone being set apart by God through your salvation. It is your family's spiritual inheritance that the entire household is chosen and set apart for His holy purposes.

Pray This:

Father in the name of Jesus we thank you for giving us the gift of salvation. We thank you that we are a called and chosen people and that you have considered us from the foundations of the world to be your people. We repent for doubting that everyone including our family members: husbands, wives and children are your people. We cast down every thought that is contrary to Your Word concerning our family sharing in the hope of glory. We cast out doubt, fear and contrary words that we have spoken against and false accusations, assumptions and judgments against our spouse's salvation. We loose the government and authority of heaven to invade my spouse soul. Father deal with my spouse until they ask, "What must I do to be saved" Father we give you glory in advance for saving, sanctifying, setting free my spouse and causing them to walk in total alignment with your word, will and ways. In Jesus Name. Amen.

Now allow your confessions (words you speak) to align with your faith and love! Unite your confessions with your prayers and marry them to your actions!

<u>Lie (14) My spouse does not appreciate me.</u>

This lie seems to affect marriages right after the **honeymoon phase** simmers down. This is a cry that is spawned by selfishness on the ends of both spouses. You are not designed to worship your spouse but worship God! When you declare that your spouse is not appreciating you and the things you do, you are asking them to admire us deeply. You are not to be worshipped by your spouse on that level of deep admiration. This is the sin of pride.

You cannot demand appreciation; you can only place a demand on ***love*** and ***submission***. Those two principles will destroy pride and ego. When you are outside of the position in love and submission; you begin to feel and create unappreciation. When you love your spouse, you will use your words to build them up thoughtfully and tell them, "That was thoughtful" and when you submit you may say, "I'm glad you have done that for me" this gracious atmosphere is far better than a place of irritation, compulsion and pride. Pride wants to be applauded for everything that has been done. Humility can do things in secret and gain rewards through blessings. However, when you follow godly order within marriage you will feel and embrace worshipping God through your humble actions toward one another and live on one accord. But, when you live your life by a worldly standard and view marriage through a secular worldview pride and ego enter and you complain of being unappreciated and *"you are not making **me** happy."* Happiness is not being defined by what your spouse does for you but what you do for self-existence. You cannot hinge appreciation and happiness on your spouse. This is an inward work of obeying the Holy Spirit and humility to receive the happiness and appreciation that you desire to feel.

Pray This:

Father in the name of Jesus, we thank you for the fruit of the spirit being an inward barometer of who we are. Father, I repent of the sins of: pride, self-idolatry and misplaced expectations. We take authority over the spirits of pride and idolatry now in the name of Jesus! We cast them out of our midst and away from our home in Jesus name. We loose love, peace, joy, hope and faith to fill every void area where pride, secular bondage and idolatry. Holy Spirit minister to my spouse and I and keep us in the spirit of truth. In Jesus Name. Amen.

Now being placing an emphasis on gratitude! Interrupt greed and anxiety, pride and ego with gratitude. Be grateful to one another and Jesus Christ. Begin to praise God aloud together and thoughtfully esteem one another for love and submission now!

Lie (15) I may as well have an affair, they understand me, my spouse stopped understanding me, believing in me, wanting me.

The enemy has the most outlandish lies and this is by far the worst one yet. First, deal with the fact that at the base of this is: *me, me, me...***Pride.** Pride is not looking to vet a need but destroy everything that you have worked for, built, separate your family and you from your children and hurt plenty of people and potentially kill the family you have created all in one—or several acts. Second, think soberly so you deliberately desire to hurt your spouse? You deliberately desire to bring depression, anger, rage and complete terror to your spouse? You like to hurt **your spouse**? That is awful. This is what is in your heart. Face it!

> *But those things, which proceed out of the mouth, come from the heart, and they defile a man. For out of the heart proceed evil thoughts, murders, adulteries, fornications, thefts, false witness, blasphemies. These are the things which defile a man, but to eat with unwashed hands does not defile a man. Matthew 15:18-20 New King James Verison.*

Your heart is deceitful and wicked. This is premeditated. Furthermore, any: unchaste conversation, illicit touch, inordinate affection for another person or *friend*, flirtatious connotations are all **premeditated**. All of these matters are what your heart desires and your natural actions and body came into agreement. Why would your heart desire to bring traumatic pain to the person you married and vowed life and fidelity to? There is something deeply terrible about this evil desire. It is wicked. It is influenced by hell and demons. If you are tempted in this manner with a person on the job, a neighbor, at church on the street... repent change your mind about yourself, your spouse and flee from this tempting person. Third, since you love yourself why in the world would you place yourself in a position to lose everything? If you love yourself why would you risk defiling your body and soul as well as the body and soul of your spouse (you are one with your spouse—you having an affair is inadvertently putting them in the bed in the act)? If you love yourself why would you disobey God and risk hell for an—or plenty of adulterous encounters that if you died you will not make heaven? If you loved yourself why would you run the risk of getting a sexually transmitted disease or infection? I have an answer. You do not love yourself this is why you are willing to run these risks. Fourth, do you love God while you desire this? When you love God, you do not desire to do anything to eschew His Presence away from you. Furthermore, do you desire curses from God? I will personally answer this for you, **NO!**

Yet ye say, Wherefore?
Because the Lord hath been witness between thee and the wife of thy youth, against whom thou hast dealt treacherously:

yet is she thy companion, and the wife of thy covenant.
And did not he make one? Yet had he the residue of the spirit.
And wherefore one? That he might seek a godly seed.
Therefore, take heed to your spirit, and let none deal treacherously against the wife of his youth.
For the Lord, the God of Israel, saith that he hateth putting away:
for one covereth violence with his garment, saith the Lord of hosts:
therefore, take heed to your spirit, that ye deal not treacherously.
Malachi 2:14-16 King James Version

Understand, when you deal treacherously with your spouse (husband or wife) of your youth (does not matter at what age or stage you have gotten married) with adultery and divorce God is definitively going to back the spouse that is "innocent" and send curses on the "guilty" spouse. You will not commit adultery and think that you will *get away with it* or that *spouse will never find out.* Why? God's eyes are on you and he sees everything that happens on this planet that **HE** created. Moreover, your spouse will feel disconnect and at the time may not have the articulation or the technology to nail you to the feeling of affair or looming affair. However, his/her discernment (inward truth) has already severed trust and is telling a story. This is the justice in this matter they deserve to go off, get angry, go through *your* stuff (in marriage there is only *community property)* and have the real truth. This requires you to put away defenses and boundaries and tell the raw truth. Be honest and get delivered from this demon that hates you, your spouse and your children and your children's children. This demonic structure wants nothing more than to *kill, steal and destroy.* Remember, divorce kills marriages and dissolves families. Adultery's ultimate goal is to separate parents from children and set up demonic infrastructures to gain hold on your legacy—your children and grandchildren. Defeat this demon today!

Pray This:

*Have mercy upon me, O God, according to thy lovingkindness:
according unto the multitude of thy tender mercies blot out my transgressions.
Wash me thoroughly from mine iniquity, and cleanse me from my sin.
For I acknowledge my transgressions: and my sin is ever before me.
Against thee, thee only, have I sinned, and done this evil in thy sight:
that thou mightiest be justified when thou speakest,
and be clear when thou judgest.
Behold, I was shapen in iniquity; and in sin did my mother conceive me.
Behold, thou desirest truth in the inward parts:
and in the hidden part thou shalt make me to know wisdom.
Purge me with hyssop, and I shall be clean: wash me, and I shall be whiter than snow.*

Make me to hear joy and gladness;
that the bones which thou hast broken may rejoice.
Hide thy face from my sins,
and blot out all mine iniquities.
Create in me a clean heart, O God;
and renew a right spirit within me.
Cast me not away from thy presence;
and take not thy holy spirit from me.
Restore unto me the joy of thy salvation;
and uphold me with thy free spirit.
Then will I teach transgressors thy ways;
and sinners shall be converted unto thee.
Deliver me from blood guiltiness, O God,
thou God of my salvation:
and my tongue shall sing aloud of thy righteousness.
O Lord, open thou my lips;
and my mouth shall shew forth thy praise.
For thou desirest not sacrifice; else would I give it:
thou delightest not in burnt offering.
The sacrifices of God are a broken spirit:
a broken and a contrite heart, O God, thou wilt not despise.
Do good in thy good pleasure unto Zion:
build thou the walls of Jerusalem.
Then shalt thou be pleased with the sacrifices of righteousness, with burnt offering and whole burnt offering:

*then shall they offer bullocks upon thine
altar.
Psalms 51*

**Breaking the Spirit of Adultery**

What to do if you find your marriage in complete shambles do to an affair? First, listen to what the Lord is saying regarding your marriage. Do not come to conclusions on your own. Do not listen to counteracting voices. When your marriage is in duress you cannot play the victim role! You must be aware and sound (sober) in your decision-making. Once you consult with heaven then agree with heaven begin to set your affections to follow suit. If God says do not divorce or separate I will bring restoration, trust me, the road will be very bumpy and hard in between time, but in the meanwhile you have to pray, fast and seek the face of God also you cannot distract your focus from God by placing your sole focus on your spouse! The adultery spouse can become a god in this situation and that hinders the healing and restoration process.

Second, you must have been keen in the spirit! Know what spirits are in operation. Is this systemic from trauma? Is this behavioral? Is this greed? Is this demonic? Get to the root cause of the affair. You will know that there will be elements of all of these questions that are at the base of the adultery. Here are prayers that I prayed that brought healing and restoration in my union.

Identifying the spirits at work in adultery: *Soul-ties* (which keeps the spouse entangled in the affair and yo-yo emotions) *Jezebel*, Delilah, Witchcraft, Adultery, Fornication, Lewdness, Lawlessness, Trauma, Grief, Betrayal, Wounded Spirit, Deception, Pride, Leviathan, Seduction, mind binding, Mind breaking, Mind Control, Lying, Sexual Addiction, Insecurity, Instability, Manipulation, Rejection, Rebellion and Abandonment and Distrust. – Prepare yourself to make war with these demons and conqueror over them. The art is to shut them down in the second heaven—this is the spiritual wickedness in high places, rulers and principalities that are consistently making war against you, your marriage, your family, your lineage, your generational blessings. Feel the aggression against these spirits. Do not, I REPEAT—DO NOT be aggressive at your spouse and do not pray/battle in front of them either, do this away from them and make it lethal. They are trying to kill you and destroy your destiny. Your spouse is still not your enemy, the demonic spirits ruling their lives and decisions are the enemy! Be prepared to annihilate what is attempting to annihilate you!

Let's pray this!

Father in the name of Jesus, I come against, bind, rebuke and cast out: *Jezebel*, Delilah, Witchcraft, Adultery, Fornication, Lewdness, Lawlessness, Trauma, Grief, Betrayal, Wounded Spirit, Deception, Pride, Leviathan, Seduction, mind binding, Mind breaking, Mind Control, Lying, Sexual Addiction, Insecurity, Instability, Manipulation, Rejection, Rebellion and Abandonment and Distrust that is operating in myself and my spouse. I dismantle, cut off, cut down and severe the soul tie between (Spouse's name/Affair partner) Your name/affair partner in Jesus name I evict (Affair partner) out of my marriage bed now in the name of Jesus. I cleanse and eradicate my marriage now of any bonds, ties, agreements, to this affair now in the name of Jesus. I sever the attraction and connection to (Affair partner) and (Spouse and Your name) now in the name of Jesus! I command any lingering affects/effects be obliterated in the second heaven now in the name of Jesus; I sprinkle the ashes of that ungodly union throughout all of the planets in the solar system to never come together again in the name of Jesus. I command Angels that are trained by Michael, legions of them come to my aide and make war, and persecute: *Jezebel*, Delilah, Witchcraft, Adultery, Fornication, Lewdness, Lawlessness, Trauma, Grief, Betrayal, Wounded Spirit, Deception, Pride, Leviathan, Seduction, mind binding, Mind breaking, Mind Control, Lying, Sexual Addiction, Insecurity, Instability, Manipulation, Rejection, Rebellion and Abandonment and Distrust in the name of Jesus! I even deal with the high places of (Spouse name) mind and command every lofty thought, prideful thought but put into captivity and the knowledge of Christ in the name of Jesus! I confront every demon of wickedness in high places that is operating (Spouses Name) to be torn down in Jesus Name! All demons of lewdness, lasciviousness, lust, and perversion are driven out of (Spouses name) sexual organs, hormones, blood, and bloodline now in the name of Jesus! Father cause (Spouses name) to be convicted by the Holy Spirit and draw (spouses name) to godly sorrow that works to repentance, cause (Spouses name) to come to themselves in the name of Jesus!

Father in the name of Jesus, I decree and declare wholeness, healing, deliverance of (Your name) and (Spouses name) cause us to come together on one accord, with nothing: missing, lacking or broken! In Jesus Name.

Also pray: Every mind binding, mind breaking, mind control spirit that is causing (spouses name) to be hypersensitive and edgy emotionally to come out of (Spouses name) now in the name of Jesus!

I cover (spouses name) in the blood of Jesus and command now that any lingering feelings and emotions are drained and rebuked now in the name of Jesus! Father your word says, "Husbands love your wives as Christ loved the church and gave himself up for her washing her with the waters of the word and wives to submit to her husband as well as, Wives your desires are to your husband only. Father cause me to feel the love of my husband, Father cause me to feel the desire of my wife in the name of Jesus. Father brings your order into our marriage and home in the name of Jesus!

I render the works of Satan powerless in my home, marriage, family and lineage now in the name of Jesus! I stop the works of adultery from falling generationally on my children from them committing adultery to experiencing the pain of adultery I command wholeness in my generations sexuality now in the name Jesus!

Understand this: we are working, travailing, crying out, binding loosing...the enemy will attack and your spouse will manifest. Read my next words carefully.... Listen to the words they are saying such as: I hate you! I want to be with (affair partner)! I am out of here! I don't think this is repairable or logical! I don't know why I am here? Why am I living? I am only here for the kids! I feel like there's no way out of the mess I have created, I should die. You deserved it! Are you done with me now?! I did this to end this marriage! I was right in having the affair you did this to yourself! I needed to get you back for what you were doing! This was the only way to get your attention! These are more ***LIES*** from Satan! Do not get distracted or discouraged by what you are hearing! Brush, it off! This is frontline war, frontline war means the enemy within your spouse has to use a tactic to try and distract you, throw you off, have you emotional, doubting, fearing and in unbelief! He knows if he has you in this manner your prayers will go unheard, unanswered and maybe even having you to distrust God because you are praying and there seems to be no results...This is the DEVIL don't listen to him! Shake it off keep toiling in prayer! Do **NOT** give in to what the enemy is saying! Even take those statements into prayer consult the Father and listen, yield to Him and do His instructions on what next move. This is usually fast and consecration time. This is the time to press more into God. Ask for mercy on your spouse, because when you are married you are tied to their judgment. So, petition God to be merciful and have grace. He will do this according to your prayers and faith. Your next move will be to shut out all of the noise from outside influences. If you have family or friends that tell you otherwise such as, "I would leave" or "I did leave" respectfully dismiss this conversation because it will interfere with your faith and seek to confuse you. Confusion is of the enemy. In this time, you need God to author and finish your faith. Allow God to write and complete your faith in this situation do not allow outside influences to write and author confusion through demonic suggestions. You may grieve not having the ability to speak with these family members or friends during this season, but that is fine. Grieve and continue on in your faith knowing that God is going to move in your home. You can endure hardship as a good solider. You are the Lord's weapon of war! You will stand and see the salvation of the Lord. The matter is going to be getting to the other side, the battle in between. You are strong enough for this war! And if you lose a battle, you will surely win the war! If your spouse refuses to leave you continue to fight and pray!

Contact Us

For speaking engagements, comments or to follow me on Social Media, contact me at:

Mailing Address
Jermael and Carrie Anthony
P.O. Box 21575
Chicago, IL 60621
P: 872.529. KHIM

Carrie's Social Media
Facebook: Carrie Betton-Anthony
Twitter: CarrieTBA
Youtube: Carrie Theresa
InstaGram: CarrieTheresaiam
SnapChat: CarrieTBA
Periscope: CarrieTBA
Linkedin: Carrie Betton-Anthony

Jermael's Social Media

www.ingramcontent.com/pod-product-compliance
Lightning Source LLC
Chambersburg PA
CBHW071946110426
42744CB00030B/514